INFORMATION GENERATION AND LIBRARY USE BY UNIVERSITY TEACHERS

INFORMATION GENERATION AND LIBRARY USE BY UNIVERSITY TEACHERS

A. DURVASA BABU

GYAN PUBLISHING HOUSE
NEW DELHI-110 002

Information Generation and Library Use by University Teachers

(Library Science, Information Science, Education, Mass Communication, Reference)

ISBN: 81-212-0461-5

Library of Congress Card No. 93-900319

Published in 1994 by
Gyan Publishing House
5 Ansari Road
New Delhi 110 002

Laser typesetting at Jeetu Graphics, Delhi- 110 094, and *printed* at Goyal Offset Works, Delhi-110 022

ACKNOWLEDGEMENTS

It gives me an immense pleasure to express my deep sense of gratitude to my revered research supervisor Prof. G.V.S.L. Narasimha Raju, Head, Department of Library and Information Science, Andhra University, Visakhapatnam, for his able guidance, constant encouragement, constructive criticism, stimulating discussions and keen interest evinced throughout the course of the present study. I am really fortunate to associate myself with such an able and experienced teacher. The help and advice rendered by him are mainly responsible for the successful completion of the present work.

I express my sincere thanks to the other faculty members of the Department of Library and Information Science, Andhra University for their constant help and cooperation.

My sincere thanks are due to Dr. K.V. Subbaraya Sarma, Reader and Head, Department of Statistics, and Dr. K. Narasimhulu, Reader, Department of Economics, Sri Venkateswara University, Tirupati, who helped me in shaping the raw-data into valuable information by the application of statistical methods.

I am thankful to Sri M.R. Chandran, Librarian, Sri Venkateswara University Library, Tirupati for his professional encouragement and liberal attitude in allowing me to pursue this work.

I express my thanks to Sri R. Sreepathi Naidu, former Librarian, Sri Venkateswara University Library for his constant encouragement in prosecuting my higher studies in enrolling for PhD. in Library and Information Science.

I am very grateful to all the teachers of Sri Venkateswara

University College of Arts and Sciences, Tirupati, who could spare their valuable time and answer my questionnaires. Without their help this investigation could not have been materialised.

My sincere thanks are also due to the authorities of Sri Venkateswara University, Tirupati who were kind enough to allow me to do my research work in Andhra University on part-time basis. I also thank the authorities of Andhra University for permitting me to register for Ph.D. in that University.

Thanks are due to my friends Mr. R.V. Gopal Rao, Mr. P. Bhaskar Rao and Mr. D. Muralidhar for their assistance at various stages during the progress of the work.

I express my thanks to the Librarian, Andhra University Library; Librarian, Sri Venkateswara University Library, Tirupati; Librarian, British Council Library, Madras; Director, USIS Information Centre, Madras; Librarian, Madras University Library, Madras and staff members of these Libraries for their help in collecting information relevant to my present study.

I offer my sincere thanks to Sri G. Munikrishna Reddy and Sri D. Venkatachalapathy for having typed the manuscript, so neatly and so elegantly.

I am highly indebted to my beloved wife and childern for their kind cooperation, affectionate encouragement and moral support which made this work possible.

CONTENTS

LIST OF TABLES

LIST OF FIGURES

LIST OF ABBREVIATIONS

AFM	:	Attitude of the Family Members
AP	:	Assistance for Publication
BCL	:	British Council Library (Madras)
BS	:	Bibliographical Service
CAS	:	Current Awareness Service
CBS	:	Chairmanship of Board of Studies
CPL	:	Connemera Public Library (Madras)
DCL	:	District Central Library
DL	:	Departmental Library
EC	:	Encouragement from Colleagues
ED	:	Education of the Dependents
EW	:	Evaluation Work
FA	:	Financial Assistance
FE	:	Faculty Environment
FJ	:	Frequent Journies Leaving Headquarters
FV	:	Frequent visits of friends and relatives
HA	:	Healthy atmosphere in the faculty
H_o	:	Null Hypothesis
HPF	:	Health Problems of the Family Members
HS	:	Headship
IGI	:	Information Generation Index

ILL	:	Inter-Library Loan
L	:	Lecturers
LF	:	Liberal Financial assistance to undertake research work
LP	:	Local Public Library
MD	:	Marriage of the Dependents
OA	:	Other Agencies of Information Sources
OAF	:	Other Academic/Official Factors
ODF	:	Other Domesitc Factors
OP	:	Off-prints
P	:	Professors
PCF	:	Personal Collection of Colleagues/friends
PHP	:	Personal Health Problems
PL	:	Personal Library
PN	:	Problems with Neighbours
PR	:	Problems with Relatives
PWC	:	Problems with Colleagues
PWH	:	Problems with Higher Officials
PWS	:	Problems with Students
R	:	Readers
REP	:	Reprographic Service
RG	:	Research Guidance
RS	:	Reference Service
RW	:	Recognition of the work
SBES	:	School of Biological and Earth Sciences
SBM	:	School of Business Management
SDI	:	Selective Dissemination of Information
SF	:	Size of the Family

SHES : School of Humanities and Extension Studies

SMPS : School of Mathematical and Physical Sciences

SRL : State Regional Library

SSBS : School of Social and Behavioural Sciences

TA : Teaching Activity

TRS : Team Research Spirit

TS : Translation Service

UL : University Library

USIS : USIS Information Centre (Madras).

PART I

THEORETICAL BACKGROUND

CHAPTER 1

INTRODUCTION

"The systematic and purposeful acquisition of information and its systematic and purposeful application are emerging as the new foundations for work, productivity and effort throughout the world."

Peter Drucker
The Age of Discontinuity,
1968

In the system of higher education, University occupy an unique place, as they function as institutions transmitting knowledge to the progeny and as research centres performing research activities and develop new ideas keeping in view the social problems and needs. Universities bear the responsibility of building the society of elites, needed for a prosperous nation. The elite group thus built includes scientists, engineers, economists, medical professionals, lawyers, agricultural scientists, etc. Thus universities play a key role in building the citizens, having the nature of free thinking, self realization and sharing the responsibility for the uplift of the society.

According to Weitz (1973)[1] any society regardless of its location in time and geography, establishes, maintains, and develops systems of education to achieve four general goals which are as follows:

1. To develop new ideas and ways of doing things that are appropriate to the changing circumstansces of the Society ;

2. To transmit these new ideas as well as the accumulated knowledge, skills, attitudes and myths of the past to the young ;

3. To facilitate the psychological growth and development of each individual student to assume a responsible and productive role in the society; and

4. To improve the quality of life in the society as a whole.

Weitz depicts the objectives, activities and functions in the figure 1. 1.

Fig. 1.1

Objectives and Functions of Higher Education

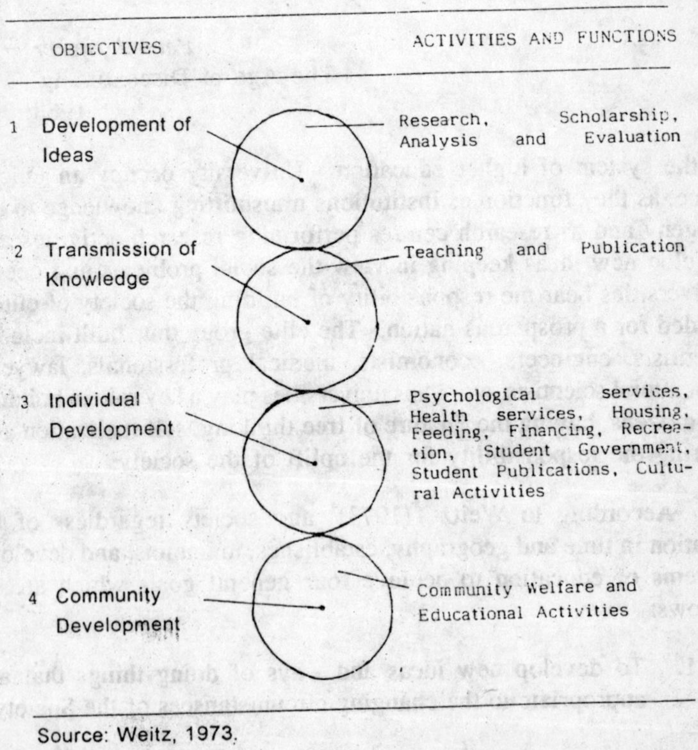

Source: Weitz, 1973.

More recently, in Western countries, and especially in the United, States the functions subsumed under objectives 1 and 2 have been differently assigned to person especially trained to carry them out. Thus, these two sets of functions have been given more unique identities although a large measure of overlap still exists.[2] But in India these two objectives and the related functions have been merged and the responsibility is fixed with the academic staff.

Teachers in Indian universities, in addition to their teaching activity, have to show some evidence for research work and also some publications in the context of promotions to higher cadres. In India, "guiding research scholars has become a profitable activity for members of university faculties, especially for the Readers and Professors. The larger the number of Ph.Ds one produces, the greater the prestige and the better are the chances of career advancement."[3] There is no discrimination in appointments such as persons involved in research activities and teachers connected with transmission of knowledge. Thus, a university teacher in India plays dual role as a teacher and as a scientist. Hence, they are called as teacher scientists.

The standard and reputation of a university is evaluated based on the performance of the academic community of that institution. The performance here means the quality and number of research projects undertaken and information generated in the form of publication of articles, text-books, monographs, submission of papers to seminars and conferences; and research guidance leading to Ph.Ds and M.Phils. Thus. The faculty members play a key role in building the image of the University.

The teacher, a vital ingredient of the university system, is the centre point of the present study. The study is primarily aimed at evaluating the performance of a teacher in the form of information generation against cadre, service and sex. Further, the study concentrates on the impact of helpful and unhelpful factors on information generation by the teacher. Such other factor, viz., library use, reading habit, etc., are also studied. The population selected for this study comes from Sri Venkateswara University College of Arts and Science, Tirupati, Andhra Pradesh. Hence, a sketch of the historical background of the Sri Venkateswara University is presented in the following section, since it is also related to this work.

Sri Venkateswara University*--Historical Background

Sri Venkateswara University named after the Lord of Seven Hills, was formally inaugurated on 2nd September, 1954. After the formation of the Andhra State, the Government desired to have a second University in the State for the advancement of higher learning. A Cabinet Sub-Committee under the Chairmanship of late Sri S.B.P. Pattabhirama Rao, the then Minister of Education, was appointed to take steps for the establishment of the University. Based on the Committee's report, the Andhra Government made arrangements for the inauguration of Sri Venkateswara University at Tirupati.

The University owes its existence to the wisdom and foresight of late Sri Tanguturi Prakasam Pantulu, the then Chief Minister of Andhra State and to them munificence of Tirumala-Tirupati Devasthanams.

The University came into existence as a teaching and affiliating University for the encouragement of higher education and research in all branches of learning, particularly in Oriental Learning. Sanskrit, Ancient Indian Arts and Culture, Architecture and Fine Arts . At the same time other subjects were not neglected. Six Post-graduate Departments in Mathematics, Physics, Chemistry, Zoology, Philosophy and Economics were started. The University College of Art and Sciences was established in 1954 and the University College of Engineering in 1959. These are the two constituent colleges run by the University.

University College of Arts and Sciences

For the last three and a half decades there has been a steady growth in the campus. The University College of Arts and Sciences expanded and diversified its courses and research activities. A number of personal and team research projects have been completed and some are also ongoing. Now the college has thirty three full-fledged departments with more than 300 faculty members and about 2,500 Post-graduate and research students.

---

*Abbreviated as S.V. University or S.V.U.

For the smooth functioning of the college, the administration was decentralised by dividing it into five schools as shown below:

1. School of Biological and Earth Sciences with six departments (SBES);

2. School of Humanities and Extension Studies with twelve departments (SHES);

3. Schools of Mathematic and Physical Sciences with four department (SMPS);

4. School of Social and Behavioural Sciences with eleven departments (SSBS); and

5. School of Business Management (SBM).

University College of Engineering

The University College of Engineering established in 1959 is offering graduate and post-graduate courses and providing research facilities leading to M.Phil. and Ph.D. degrees. Part-time courses are also offered for the diploma holders who can not prosecute their regular higher studies due to their jobs or some other activities.

Institute of Correspondence Courses

For the benefit of those students who do not get admission in regular studies and also for those who are doing some jobs and in order to encourage them to pursue their higher studies through private study the University established the Institute of Correspondence Courses which offer M.Com., M.A. in Economic, English, Political Science, Public Administration and Telugu, M. Sc., in Mathematics, and B.A. with various combinations. Some courses leading to Diplomas and Certificates are also offered. To provide reading facilities for the private and non-residential students, the University also opened Study Centres at Anantapur, Chittoor, Cuddapah, Kavali, Kurnool, Nellore and Tirupati.

Oriental Research Institute

Sri Venkateswara University Oriental Research Institute was started by the Tirumala-Tirupati Devasthanams in 1938 exclusively for Oriental Studies. Primary importance was given to Sanskrit. However later Telugu and Tamil were also included for undertaking research in Prabandha and Vaishnava Sampradaya literature. In November, 1956, the Institute was transferred from the Devasthanams to the S. V. University for better utilisation of the resources. Now, the Institute occupies a pride place among the few institutions of India devoted to the cause of Oriental Studies.

Post graduate Centre

The University has three Post-graduate centres established at Cuddapah, Kavali and Kurnool, offering Post-graduate courses in Commerce, Economics, Public Administration, Chemistry, Physics, Geology, Zoology, Operations Research and Satistical Quality Control and Telugu. Research facilities leading to M.Phil and Ph.D. are also available in these centres.

Objectives of the Study

The study is based on the following main objectives :

1. To study information generation among Professors, Readers and Lecturers and to find the relation between cadres and information generation;

2. To examine the relation between the teaching experience and the information generated by the teachers;

3. To find out the impact of sex on information generation by university teaching community;

4. To examine the influence of faculty environment, financial assistance and recognition of the work on information generation by academic community;

5. To study the impact of domestic factors such as family problems, Personal problems, etc. in obstructing the information generation by University teachers;

6. To study the impact of academic and official factors viz., headship, teaching activity, research guidance and problems from colleagues and higher officials, etc., in obstructing the information generation by the University teachers;

7. To find out the information agencies used by the University teachers in collecting information required for teaching and research activities;

8. To find out the awareness of various library services among the University teachers; and

9. To examine the relation between the time spent in reading documents and the generation of information.

Based on the aforementioned objectives the following hypotheses have been drafted for this work:

1. Information generation by way of writing articles to journals, seminar and conference papers, monographs and by way of guiding research and producing Ph.Ds. and M.Phils., is uniform among all cadres of the University teachers.

2. Information generation is not directly proportional to the teaching experience of the teacher.

3. Sex factor has the major role to play in information generation, i.e., both men and women faculty members are not equally good at information generation.

4. Faculty environment like team spirit among the colleagues, encouragement and healthy atmosphere in the departments will not help generate new information by the teaching community.

5. Financial assistance for research and academic work is not an important factor in information generation by the University teaching community.

6. Recognition for work is not a helpful factor in the generation of new information by the University teaching community.

7. Personal and domestic factor like health, family commitments, interaction with visitor, and neighbours do not come in the way of generation of new information by the University teachers.

8. Administrative and academic burdens and problems will not hamper the generation of new information by the University teaching community.

9. For generation of new information, University teachers need not depend mainly on the University library, but make use of other library centres and personal collections.

10. University teachers who generate new information may not be aware of usefulness of the library and its services.

11. University teachers who generate new information cannot spend more time in reading consulting documents.

Scope of the Study

The study is confined to the teachers working in Sri Venkateswara University College of Arts and Sciences, Tirupati. A sample is selected from the teachers of all cadres who are involved in teaching and research.

In order to quantify the information generation by the teaching community, only the formal type of information generation like articles, seminar papers, etc., are taken into consideration. Though they also form part of the information generation, oral and conventional forms, viz., classroom notes, are not taken into consideration, because it is felt that authentic data may not be forthcoming. As such in the study, the concept 'informationgeneration' is concerned with the publications only, viz., published articles, books, papers presented at conferences and seminars and research works leading to Ph.Ds. and M.Phils ' and Research Projects.

Limitations of the Study

The act of information generation is not equal to the act of creation which is "an original production of human intelligence"[4] and "produced through imaginative skills"[5] in its concept. But involvement of human thinking, intelligence and psychology are seen with both the activities. Hence, impact of the conditions prevailing in the surroundings play an important role either in encouraging or hampering these activities. In this context both the terms for this study are considered equal and the term creativity' is freely used in the sense of information generation. Relevant references on creativity are also quoted at appropriate places in the study wherever found meaningful.

1. For purpose of consideration of papers published in professional journals no distinction is made between individual contribution and contribution in collaboration with others. The reasons are :

   (*i*) it is felt that it will be difficult for the respondents to give the correct data over a period of years; and

   (*ii*) it will be difficult for the respondents to differentiate clearly what his contribution is and what his collaborator's contribution is.

2. Marital life, that is year of marriage and number of children was also intended to be a part of the study and thus was included it in the questionnaire. It was intended to find out the productivity of the university teachers prior to marriage and after the marriage. This information which was felt could be obtained through the bio-data of the respondents, was not forthcoming as the respondents could not provide the bio-data.

3. Among the respondents only a very few were possessing foreign qualifications (Professors-2; Readers-3; Lecturers-0). The number was however in sufficient to make out any purposeful study.

4. It was found difficult to quantify the utility of the library services. Hence, only awareness of library services among the university teachers was counted.

5. The data was collected during the months of October, November and December of 1990. As such information generation of each teacher for this study would end with 1990.

Methodology

The study is mainly based on the primary data collected from the teaching community through a well designed questionnaire. In this process of collecting the data, teachers were interviewed personally to cover the gaps in the questionnaire and to clear their doubts. Besides, the secondary data was collected from sources like text books, reference books and national and international journals and magazines.

Development of the Questionnaire and Collection of Data

The data was collected by using empirical methods of questionnaire and interview. To collect the data precisely, the Investigator employed the two methods in order to check the set-backs if any.

At first, a pilot study was conducted to test the feelings of the respondents in answering the questions. Then the well tested questionnaire was distributed personally to the teachers department-wise among the five schools of the University College of Arts and Sciences, Tirupati. Sufficient time was given to the respondents in furnishing the information. At the time of collecting the filled questionnaire each respondent was requested to offer his comments and opinions on various concepts included in it. Their suggestions relating to the improvement of library services were also called for.

Selection of the Sample

Academic community of the University includes Professors, Readers and Lecturers, who are involved in teaching on the one hand and research activity on the other. S.V. University College of Arts and Sciences and S.V. University College of Engineering are under the direct management of S.V. University situated at Tirupati in the State of Andhra Pradesh. All cadres of faculty members working in S.V.U. College of Arts and Sciences were taken into account for the Present study. The population structure is as follows.

(i)	Professors	75
(ii)	Readers	108
(iii)	Lecturers	118

The break up of the Population as per school-wise, cadre-wise and sex-wise is presented in Table 1.1.

Table 1.1
Break up of the Population

School	*Professors*		*Readers*		*Lecturers*		*Total*	
	M	*F*	*M*	*F*	*M*	*F*	*M*	*F*
SBES	18	-	12	8	16	9	46	18
SHES	19	-	29	2	23	4	71	6
SMPS	16	1	21	1	17	-	54	2
SSBS	18	-	29	1	37	6	84	7
SBM	3	-	5	-	6	-	14	-
Total	74	1	96	12	99	19	269	32

Note : M=Male; F=Female.

Source : S.V. University College of Arts and Sciences, Calender and Hand Book, 1990-91.

The total population of teachers in the college irrespective of cadre and sex is 301. Among them 75 (24.9 percent are) Professors, of them only one is the lady Professor from SMPS. There are 108 Readers whose percentage is 35.8. Among them 12 (12.5 percent) are females. Of 118 Lecturers (39.2 percent), 19 (19.19 percent) belong to female sex. On the whole there are 269 male teachers (89.36 percent) and 32 female teachers (10.63 percent).

Selection of the sample needs a high skill as it is a complicated process. In this study, Random Sampling technique was employed for the selection of the sample. In order to see that the survey is more effective, 50 percent of the University teachers were taken as a sample for the study. Since the population has three different strata, viz., Lecturers, Readers and Professors, the method of Stratified Random Sampling with 50 percent of units from each stratum was employed.

Based on the Stratified Random with 50 percent in each category altogether 38 Professors, 54 Readers and 59 Lecturers were chosen as respondents for the study.

A pilot survey regarding the attitude of the teachers towards response to the study resulted in a reduction in the number of Professors under the sample. To compensate for this an increase in the cadre of Readers and Lecturers was made and the total sample was slightly higher than 50 percent of the population. The sample size in each category is as follows :

Professors	29 (38.7 percent)
Readers	58 (53.7 percent)
Lecturers	72 (64.2 percent)

Figures in parentheses indicate percentages against population in the concerned cadres. The break-up of the sample on the basis of cadre, sex and service is shown in detail, in the analysis part of the present study.

Scoring Design

A specially structured five-point gradation is designed and employed to measure the information generation by the University teaching community, called 'Information Generation Index' (IGI). The IGI used is shown in Table 1.2.

Table 1.2
IGI - Five-Point Gradation Table

Sl. No.	Type of Information Generated	Points Assigned
1.	Ph.D. awarded	5
2.	Ph.D. submitted	4
3.	M. Phil. awarded	4
4.	M. Phil. submitted	3
5.	Article published in foreign journal	3
6.	Aritcle accepted for publication in foreign journal	2
7.	Article published in Indian journal	2
8.	Article accepted for publication in Indian journal	1
9.	Conference and Seminar papers presented in foreign country	3
10.	Accepted in foreign country	2
11.	Presented in India	2
12.	Accepted in India	1
13.	Book Published	5
14.	Book in press	4
15.	Personal research project	4
16.	Joint research project	3

For the item 'Reasons for Seeking Information' where the respondents were requested to give their personal choice of priority, a seven point scale was designed.

The following aspects were considered for reasons in order to seek information :

1. To prepare for class room;
2. General awareness of new knowledge;
3. For participation in Seminars/Conferences, etc.;
4. To meet the needs of the promotional opportunities;
5. To generate new information out of curiosityan inquisitiveness;
6. To write text books; and
7. Any other reason (please specify).

For the 1st priority the largest score 7 was given and 6, 5, 4, 3, 2, 1 were given for 2nd, 3rd, 4th, 5th, 6th, and 7th priorities respectively.

For the item 'Helpful Factors for Information Generation, the following aspects were considered :

1. Healthy atmosphere in the faculty;
2. Encouragement from colleagues;
3. Help by way of liberal finances to undertake research;
4. Team Research Spirit;
5. Assistance for Publication;
6. Recognition of the work; and
7. Any other (please specify).

The respondents were asked to give priority of their choice. Only those factors given 1st priority were taken to study the significance of relation between the factors and cadre in information generation. These factors were divided into three major groups. They are :

(a) Faculty Environment : which included :

(i) Healthy Atmosphere in the faculty (HA);

(ii) Encouragement from Colleagues (EC);

(iii) Team Research Spirti (TRS).

(b) Financial Assistance : which included :

(i) Help by way of Liberal Finance to undertake research (LF);

(ii) Assistance for Publication (AP). ;

(c) Recognition of the Work (RW).

For the other items, viz., unhelpful factors (A and B), sources for seeking information and awareness of library services only positive responses were taken as they were framed on 'Yes' or 'No' type of questions. Need of scoring was not felt, as the percentages were found self-explanatory.

Statistical Techniques Employed

The data collected through the questionnaire was analysed by employing the following statistical techniques :

Chi-square test was used to compare an observed group of frequencies with an expected group of frequencies. This led to deduce the expected frequencies from the null hypothesis.

Coefficient of Dispersion, Properties of Median, Precentages, Averages, Scaling methods were the other techniques used for the extension of the analysis of data and to draw some inferences.

Plan and Design of the Study

The study is mainly organised into two parts, namely :

Part I: Theoretical Background, and

Part II: Analysis of Data.

Part I is divided into the following five chapters keeping in view the objectives of the study.

Introduction is the subject matter for the first chapter. It provides information on the objectives and hypotheses of the study in detail. It also includes limitations of the study and methodology adopted in the collection and analysis of the data.

Second chapter deals with some of the various definitions of information and its nature.

Third chapter deals with the modes of information generation and the factors influencing the act of information generation.

Fourth chapter is devoted to the information generation by academic community. It also deals with the factors influencing the information generation.

Fifth chapter is confined to the information needs and means of acquiring information, the agencies of information used by the academic community.

Part II of this study dealing with analysis of the collected data is divided into the following four chapters.

Sixth chapter deals with the analysis part of the data related to information generation by the university teachers in relation with cadre, service and sex. It also includes the origin of inspiration for information generation.

Seventh chapter is mainly concerned with the analysis part of the data related to factors influencing information generation, which includes helpful factors, viz., faculty environment, financial assistance, recognition of the work and unhelpful factors like domestic factors and academic and official factors.

Eighth chapter examines and studies the analysis part of the data related to agencies of information used by the university academic community, awareness of library services, time spent in reading and reasons for seeking information. At the end, an analysis of suggestions received (related to library service) from teachers is presented.

Ninth chapter comprises findings and conclusions. It also provides some recommendations relating to the library services and areas of further research followed by a select bibliography.

REFERENCES

1. Weitz, Henry, Some Observations on the Objectives of Students, Services in Indian Colleges and universities. *In* Parker, Clyde A. (Ed.) Selected readings in student services for Indian Universities and Colleges, New Delhi : U.S. Educational Foundation in India, 1973, pp. 333-334.
2. *Ibid.*, p. 337.
3. Sundaram, P.S., At What Cost? *The Hindu,* 24. Dec. 1991.
4. The Shorter Oxford English Dictionary on Historical Principles, Oxford : Clarendon Press, 1973, Vol.1, p. 452.
5. Webster's Seventh New College Dictionary, 2nd ed., Calcutta: Scientific Book Agency, 1971, p. 195.

CHAPTER 2

INFORMATION AND ITS NATURE

Information-Ideas and Concepts

"Information is the product of the human brain in action and may be abstract or concrete, e.g., love, fear or book, pen. When an individual begins to think, a variety of images and sensations flash through his mind."[1] Further, some other scientists have correlated information and energy, viz., "information is a commodity no less tangible than energy; if anything, it is more pervasive in human affairs."[2]

Ducker (1969) compares information with that of electricity and expresses, "Information like electricity, is a form of energy... information is energy for mind work."[3]

"Information, in one form or another, has consistently been a significant element in the development of human society and that it has shaped, over a long period of time, the way in which we think and act."[4] It has become ingredient of man's life cycle and such that there is no life in the modern society without information. Information has become an essential commodity for the man to perform his day-to-day duties. Information is a resource of immense economic and social value. It is vital to the proper functioning of a democratic society, a crucial tool in a productive economy and an effective government, a central part of the growth and well-being of individuals.

What is Information ?

Until 1965, no definition was found for the term 'Information'. The participants of a working group at a symposium on education for information science [5] came to a conclusion that "information is a category word, for there are many kinds of information" and defined information as "recorded marks". Information is thought to be imbedded in the recorded signs which can be extracted by suitable processes.

The study of the history of the word 'information' includes examination of its origin, the way in which it has been defined and used over time and compilation and analysis of the way in which the term is presently defined and applied in various disciplines. Non-specialists use the term information in a broad sense. Anglo-American legal profession has had a highly specialised meaning for the term information since the Fifteenth century. "It is only in the Twentieth century that other professions and disciplines have begun to use the term in specialised ways to reflect the interests and needs of a particular field of study."[6]

A lot of work has been done on the history of information—its development and the definition of the term based on its evolution. In their studies, J. Campbell (1982),[7] C. Cherry (1951)[8] and Y. Bar-Hillel (1955)[9] have elaborately touched the historical and evolution aspects of the term 'information'. There are other significant general works made by Cherry (1978)[10] D. Nauta (1972) [11] and F.I. Dretske (1981).[12] According to Stevens, "Cherry has done an outstanding job of examining, surveying and summarizing the literature and concepts of a very broad field. The works of Nauta and Dretske are specialised as they seek to present complex arguments to a specialised audience. Dretske approaches the subject from the stand—point of a philosopher interested in clarifying the meaning of the concept of information by examining the fundamental ideas of communication theory, by analysing the idea of information in the context of questions relating to the theory of knowledge, and by considering a number of complex issues relating to belief, concepts and meaning. Nauta, on the other hand, approaches the subject of the meaning of information from the standpoint of semiotics. His work is, by far, the best approach to understanding term the from a linguistic, semantic and philosophical standpoint that has been published to date."[13]

Whittemore and Yovits (1973) defined the term information as "data of value to decision-making."[14]

According to Bell (1979) information is news, facts, statistics, reports, legislation, tax codes, judcial decisions, resolutions and the like.[15]

`Mikhailov et.al (1966) have cited Brillouin's definition.[16]

"Information is the raw-material and consists of a mere collection of data."

They have defined information as "the objective content of the link between interacting material objects, which reveals itself in the transformed status of these objects."

Mc Donough (1963)[17] states that "Information is the measure of the net value obtained from the process of matching the elements of a present problem with appropriate elements of data." He further states that "information ... is a process which occurs within a human mind when a problem and data useful for its solution are brought into productive union." This shows that information is the product of human thinking caused when the problems are solved using the data related to it.

Hayes (1969) defines information as the "result of data, usually formalized in processing."[18] Here also a relation between the human mind or thinking and the processing of data supplied is seen. On this definition Hans Wellisch (1972) comments that "although operational on certain level, again seems to leave out what goes on in the mind of a person informed and stresses the mechanistic aspect of processing, although information is here no longer considered as a kind of physical substance."[19]

Otten and Debons (1970) state that "information is a fundamental phenomenon like energy, on which operations can be performed. They further view that "all information processing operations can be performed by digital computers."[20]

Wersig (1970) defines information as "reduction of uncertainty."[21]

According to Shera (1970) information is a 'fact'. "It is the stimulus which we perceive through our senses. This information may be a single isolated fact or it may be a whole cluster of facts; but it is still a unit; it is a unit of thought. It can have any dimension. It is that intellectual entity which we receive, the building block of knowledge."[22]

Mackay (1969) states that "we may define information in general as that which justifies representational activity."[23] Here the words, representational activity imply anything a person can say, write or signal to other persons.

Davis (1974) has defined information as "data that has been processed into a form that is meaningful to the recipient and is of real perceived value in current or prospective decision."[24]

Stevens (1986) has defined the information as "the factual data, ideas and other knowledge emanating from any segment of society that are identified as being of value, sometimes gathered on a regular basis, organized in some fashion, transmitted to others and used in some meaningful fashion."[25]

In Webster's Third New International Dictionary the term 'information' is defined as "the communication or reception of knowledge or intelligence; something obtained or received through informing; the process by which the form of an object of knowledge is impressed upon the apprehending mind so as to bring about the status of knowing."[26]

Fairthrone (1967) says that "information is a metaphorical designation for an amorphous mass of ill-defined different activities and phenomena." [27] Further, he thinks "information as the name of some stuff. This substance is squeezed from books like water from sponge and can be stored and pumped around."[28]

Information and Knowledge are often used synonymously. There is a difference. Information may be a single fact or many unrelated facts, whereas knowledge is an ordered and structured information.

Kent (1979) states that "informations is the feed stock for knowledge. In an idea world of unimpeded flow of information amongst individuals of equal capacity to process the information into knowledge there would be no advantage to be gained by any individual or group as compared with another by possession of information."[29]

Goffman (1970) expresses that as the definitions of information are not clear and vary from the expressions of one scientist to the other, the study should be made on the information related phenomena rather than information.[30]

Brookes says that knowledge is a sum of many bits of information and when more information is added to the existing knowledge structure, it gets modified. When information $\Delta 1$ is added to the existing body of knowledge K(S), it results in modified knowledge $K(S + \Delta S)$. This can be represented as $K(S) + \Delta 1 = K(S + \Delta S)$.[31]

Machlup and Mansfield (1983) have defined information by differentiating it from that of knowledge.

According to them :

(i) Information is piece-meal, fragmented and particular, whereas knowledge is structural, coherent and universal;

(ii) Information is timely, transitory, perhaps even ephimeral, whereas knowledge is of enduring significance;

(iii) Information is a flow of message, whereas knowledge is a stock largely resulting from the flow, in the sense that the input of information may affect the stock of knowledge by added to it, restructuring it or changing it in any way (though conceivably information may leave knowledge unchanged).[32]

In 'Elsevier's Dictionary of Library Science, Information and Documentation', information is explained as "the meaning that a human assigns to data by means of the known conversation used in its representation."[33]

The Concise Encyclopaedia of Information Technology simply states information as "the meaning attached to data."[34]

Whereas in the Oxford English Dictionary[35], information is taken as a verb and the following meanings are given :

(*i*) Communication of instructive knowledge.

(*ii*) Communication of knowledge or news of some fact or occurrence.

(*iii*) Knowledge communicated concerning some particular fact, subject or event.

Further, Buckland (1991)[36] distinguishes three meanings of 'information' by analysing the dictionary meanings given in the Oxford English Dictionary, 1989.

(*a*) **Information-as-process** : When some one is informed, what they know is changed. In this sense "information" is "The act of informing...; Communication of the knowledge or 'new' of some fact or occurrence; the action of telling or fact of being told of something."

(*b*) **Information-as-knowledge** : 'Information' is also used to denote that which is perceived in 'information-as-process; the "Knowledge communicated concerning some particular fact, subject or event; that of which one is appraised or told; intelligence, news."

(*c*) **Information-as-thing** : The term 'information' is also used attributively for objects, such as data and documents, that are referred to as 'information' because they are regarded as being informative, as 'having the quality of imparting knowledge or communicating information; instructive."

Putting together various definitions of the scientists it can be expressed that information is processed data of value; produced by any segment of the society. As and when more information is added to the existing knowledge structure, it gets modified. In other words, it can be said that information is the feed stock for knowledge. Information is flow of messages in piece-meal or fragments having the nature of timeliness and transitory.

Nature of Information

Information is the knowleged put to use, which may produce good or bad results. The value of information is in the hands of the manager, or scientist or any person concerned with decision-making to use the information on hand in a prospective way.

No decision is generally taken in the midst of uncertain options. Here, it is the information that helps the decision-maker arrive at a decision by reducing the uncertainty. Prasher puts that "the degree of uncertainty, however, varies from person to person depending on the time and place."[37] As such the quantity of information required for taking decisions varies from person to person depending on the situation, speed with which the decision is to be taken and the place where the decision is to be taken.

The nature and amount of information that affects the behaviour of a person (*i.e.*, recipient) in taking the decision, however, varies from person to person, from time to time, and from place to place. As such 'information is a resource of immense economic and social value. It is vital to the proper functioning of a democratic society, a crucial tool in a productive economy and also for an effective government, a central part of the growth and well-being of individuals."[38]

The increasing need and dependence on information and the increase in technological sophistication and the complexities of modern social life have increased its nature and value. The nature and value of information is directly related to its communication. "Information communicated could be broadly grouped into three categories : (1) developmental (2) pedagogic, and (3) achievemental; when one uses a document for general cultural advancement for enlargement of his vision, and for intellectual enjoyment, the information obtained is developmental; when a student studies a prescribed text-book or refers to an index, with a view to supplement the instruction the information communicated is pedagogic; and if a scientist working in a laboratory refers to abstracts and indexes relating to the field of investigation or experiment, the information received is achievemental in quality."[39]

Burt Nanun (1981)[40] explains that information has peculiar properties, which make it very difficult to generalize about it. For instance :

(*a*) It is not homogeneous like electricity or grain, but rather is extremely heterogeneous, with virtually infinite variation in response to individual conjunctions of supplier, processor, user and channel of communication.

(*b*) It is rarely of value in itself, but rather requires a context, structure, or model within which it can be interpreted.

(*c*) Demand for information is a function of such variables as age, perishability, convenience, reliability, source etc., as well as more traditional economic variables such as cost quantity and availability of supply.

(*d*) The role of information in an organization is so central to its management and functioning that it must be viewed as a fundamental factor of production like money and man-power.

(*e*) Both suppliers and users of information often need special protection by means of government intervention such as copy right and patent laws, privacy legislation and fraud statutes.

Information is a social process—its nature and value are closely related to the information needs and approaches of information. Wersig and Neveling (1975)[41] account the following approaches of information based on which the nature of the information can be assessed :

(*i*) **The Structural Approach.** In this approach information— is viewed as structure of the world or static relations between physical objects which may be perceived or not.

(*ii*) **The Knowledge Approach.** This approach records knowledge that is built on the basis of perception of the structure of the world. But the problem with this approach is that the term 'information' any erroneously be used for term 'know/ ledge'.

(*iii*) **A Message Approach.** The mathematical theory of communication uses this approach. It is concerned with the transmission of symbols representing a message.

(*iv*) **The Meaning Approach.** In this approach the semantic-content of a message is accepted as information.

Koblitz (1969)[42] distinguishes three kinds of information with which we can note the nature of information at various stages being used in the society. The three kinds of information are :

(*i*) "Semantic Information" (as a message) is a unit composed of meaning and carrier for the purpose of transmission of knowledge and experience from one subject to another." Here, the information is having the nature of a message. In this process, information has clear meaning and transmitted the knowledge and experience of one person to the other. This is a never ending process and widely seen in the society.

(*ii*) "Semantic Information" (as a process) is of purposeful action for the creation (including handling), storage, searching and dissemination of information and coupled with sensory perception (unilateral), logical perception (inner reflection) or exchange of information between humans (bilateral)."

(*iii*) "Documental Information" which is "information containing new factors or statements of analytical or synthetic character." The nature of documental information is of facts or statements which have analytical or synthetic character. And these facts and statements are supported by evidences. Koblitz also called it factographic information.

Bhattacharya (1978)[43] expresses that information has its varieties, which are recognizable on the basis of different characteristics, falling under two universally recognizable varieties :

(*a*) Discursive information, and

(*b*) Non-discursive information.

According to him 'Discursive Information' is the message conveyed by a systematized body of ideas or its accepted or acceptable substitutes, having one or more of the following attributes relating to its treatment or expression :

(*a*) Ranging over a wide field;

(*b*) Proceeding logically or coherently from topic to topic; and

(*c*) Reasoning from premises to conclusion; or proceeding from particulars to generalization utilizing or based upon analytical reasoning; or proceeding from logical abstraction to logical interpretation.

On the other hand a message consisting of a unit or atomic fact conveyed by a systematized body or its accepted or acceptable substitutes is 'Non-discursive Information :

Non-discursive Information is of two types :

(*i*) Qualitative; and

(*ii*) Quantitative.

The relationships among different varieties of information are very close—one variety of information forming the base for the other variety. Information is a resource, viewed from the point of its effect. "It is a direct input to the process of generation of new information, decision-making and deriving emotional satisfaction.

Indirectly, it is an input to the process of production of commodities and service. More specifically, information is an energy resource; for, it is intended to initiate desired actions."[44]

Melvin J. Voigt (1962)[45] made the analysis of the composite nature of information based on the user's approach to information. The nature of information is closely related to the approach of the user based on time, purpose in relation to his work, stage of his work, general interest, amount of information already available, etc. The approaches to information are : (*i*) Current approach, (*ii*) Everyday approach, and (*iii*) Exhaustive approach.

The need for information differs from person to person and the many roles they daily assume viz., worker, parent, citizen, decision-maker, patient, teacher, consumer, judge, etc. Moreover, information is a strange commodity, although it has definable costs of production and distribution, it is of undeniable value to a user.

Burt Nanun says that "the problem of assessing user needs in the future is further exacerbated by the fact that the environment of user needs is rapidly changing. Virtually, everything in the social environment affects user needs and in turn is affected by information usage.[46]

Some scientists have correlated the nature of information with that of energy. In his definition, McCarthy (1966) states that "information is a commodity no less tangible than energy; if any thing, it is more pervasive in human affairs."[47] Another definition given by Drucker (1969) compares "information like electricity, is a form of energy ... information is energy for mind work."[48] Wiener (1954) discussed relationships between information and energy. According to him, "information is a name for the content of what is exchanged with the outer world as we adjust to it, and make our adjustment felt upon it ... The transfer of information cannot take place without a certain expenditure of energy, so that there is no sharp boundary between energetic coupling and information coupling."[49]

Rathswol (1975)[50] states that the nature of information is generally talked in terms of four concepts-commodity, process, state of knowing-and environment and that two approaches have been taken in each case definitional and criterial. According to Rathswol there are four concepts of information and they are :

(*a*) **Commodity.** This concept refers to the empirical content of communications and knowledge. Information as a commodity represents some thing, e.g., some event, some state of the world.

(*b*) **Process.** This concept refers to the structural and organizational aspects of communications and knowledge. Information as a process is represented by something, e.g., genetic structure.

(*c*) **State of Knowing.** This concept relates directly to the effect of information in terms of changes in a human knower. Information as a state of knowing relates directly to the structural - functional aspects of human knowing activity.

(*d*) **Environment.** This concept refers to man-machine and man -man systems, etc., command and control systems, within which certain data—information transformations occur.

Rathswol has adopted the two approaches for understanding the concept of information—definitional approach and criterial approach.

Definitional Approach — The definitional approach is an attempt to offer a definition of information; the approach is oriented towards explicating the meaning of information.

Criterial Approach — The criterial approach is an attempt to specify the test-conditions for determining whether or not certain commodities, processes, states, or environments could be characterized as information, e.g, under what conditions would one be able to recognise this commodity as information commodity ?

From these studies the following inference can be drawn. The nature of information is related with the mode of its generation and its utility. On the other side, use of information is based on the needs of the users and their methods of approach, which are instigated and controlled by the social changes that are taking place and the social problems to be solved. Solutions found to solve these problems, will ultimately lead to generation of new information.

REFERENCES

1. Viswanathan, C.G., Elements of Information Science, New Delhi : Today and Tomorrow Printers and Publishers, 1976, p. 2.
2. McCarthy, J., Information. *In* Information : A Scientific American Book, San Francisco : W.H. Freeman and Co., 1966, p.1.
3. Drucker, P.F., The Age of Disconinutity : Guidelines to our Changing Society, New York : Harper and Row, 1969, p.27.
4. Stevens, Norman D., The History of Information. *In* Advances in Librarianship, Vol. 14, Edited by Wesley Simonton, Orlando Academic Press, 1986, p. 2.
5. Symposium on Education for Information Science, Warrenton, Washington, D.C. : Spartan Books, 1965, p. 171.
6. Stevens, Norman D., *op.cit.*, p.6.
7. Campbell, J., Grammatical Man, New York : Simon and Schustar, 1982.
8. Cherry, C., A History of the Theory of Information, *Proceedings of the Institute of Electrical Engineer,* 98, 1951, pp. 383-393.
9. Bar-Hillel, Y., An Examination of Information Theory, *Philosophy of Science,* 22, 1955, pp. 86-105.
10. Cherry, C., On Human Communication, Cambridge : Massachusetts, M.I.T. Press, 1978.
11. Nauta, D., The Meaning of Information, The Hague : Mouton, 1972.
12. Dretske, F.I., Knowledge and Flow of Information, Cambridge : Massachusetts, M.I.T. Press, 1981.
13. Stevens, Norman D., *op.cit.*, p.7.
14. Whittemore, B.C., and Yovits, M.C., A Generalised Conceptual Development for the Analysis of Information., *Journal of American Society for Information,* 24(3), 1973, pp. 221-231.
15. Bell, D., Social Frame-work of Information Theory. *In* Dertouzos, M.L. and Moses (Ed). The Computer Age, A Twenty Year View, Cambridge : M.I.T. Press, 1979, pp. 163-211.
16. Mikhailov, A.I., Chernyi, A.I. And Gilyarevskii. Informatics - New Name for the Theory of Scientific Communication (Nanko-tekhnicheskaya informatisya, No. 12, 1966, pp. 35-39) English translation in *FID News Bulletin,* Vol. 17, 1967, pp. 70-74.

17. McDonough, A.M., Information, Economics and Management Systems, New York : McGraw Hill, 1963. Quoted by Hoshovsky, A.G. and Massey, R.J., Information Science—Its ends, means and opportunities. *In* : Information Transfer, *Proc. American Society for Information Science,* Vol. 5, 1968, pp. 47-55.
18. Hayes, R.M., Information is Librarianship, *Libri,* 19(3), 1969, pp. 216-236 (Published in Hayes, R.M. and Becker, J., Handbook of Data Processing for Libraries, New York : Wiley, 1970, Chapter-20.
19. Wellish, Hans., From Information Science to Informatics, *Journal of Librarianship,* 4(3), 1972, p. 173.
20. Otten, K. and Debons, A., Towards a Meta-science of Information : Informatology, *Journal of American Society for Information Science,* 21(1), 1970, pp. 89-94.
21. Wersig, G. and Meyer, Uhlenried, K.H., Versuche Zur Terminologic in der Dokumentation III : Dokumentation, Nachr. *Dokum,* 22(1), 1970, pp. 14-19.
22. Shera, J.H., Sociological Foundations of Librarianship, New York : Asia Publishing House, 1970.
23. Mackay, D.M., Information, Mechanism and Meaning, Cambridge, Mass: M.I.T. Press, 1969.
24. Davis, G.B., Management Information Systems, New York : McGraw-Hill, 1974, p. 32.
25. Stevens, Norman D., *op.cit.,* p. 9.
26. Webster, N., Third New International Dictionary, Merriam : Springfield, Massachusetts, 1978, p. 1160.
27. Fairthrone, R.A., Morphology of Information Flow, *Journal of Association for Computing Machinery,* 14, 1967, pp. 710-719.
28. Fairthrone, R.A., Information : One Label, Several Bottles. *In* : Debons, Anthony and Camerom, William J. (Ed.), Perspectives in Information Science, Leyden : Noordhoff International Publishing, 1975, p. 67.
29. Kent, A.K., Information as Power. *ASLIB Proceedings,* 31(1), 1979, p. 16.
30. Goffman, W., Information Science : Discipline or Disappearance, *ASLIB* Proceedings, 22(12), 1970, pp. 589-596.
31. Brookes, B.C., Foundation of Information Science. *Journal of Information Science,* 2(3-4), 1980, pp. 125-33, pp. 209-221. pp. 269-275; 3(1), 1981, pp. 3-12.
32. Machlup, F. and Mansfield, U., Study of Information Interdisciplinary Messages. New York : Wiley, 1983, p. 743.
33. Calson, W.E. (Comp), Elsevier's Dictionary of Library Science, Information and Documentation. Amsterdam : Elsevier Scientific Publishing Company, 1976, p. 207.

34. Stoker, Adrain, V., Concise Encyclopaedia of Information Technology, 2nd ed. Brookfield (USA): Gower Publishing Company, 1985, p. 114.
35. The Oxford English Dictionary, Oxford : The Clarendon Press, 1989, Vol. 7, p. 944.
36. Buckland, Michael K., Information as Thing. *Journal of the American Society for Information Science,* 42(5), 1991, p. 351.
37. Prasher, R.G., Information and Its Communication, *ILA Bulletin,* XXIII(3), October-December 1987, p. 96.
38. Public Sector/Private Sector Interaction in Providing Information Services, report of National Commission on Libraries and Information Science, February, 1982. Cited by Wilson, Alex. The Information Rich and the Information Poor. *ASLIB Proceedings,* 39(1), 1987, p.1.
39. Viswanathan C.G., *op.cit.,* p. 5.
40. Nanun, Burt., "User Needs for Information in Year 2000". *In :* Boaz, Martha., "Strategies for Meeting the Information Needs of Society in the Year 2000". Littleton Colorado : Libraries Unlimited Inc., 1981, p. 56.
41. Wersig, G. and Neveling, U., Phenomena of Interest to Information Science, *Information Science,* 9(4), 1975, pp. 127-140.
42. Koblitz. J., Librarianship and Documentation Information : Distinctive Features and Common Aspects. *In :* On Theoretical Problems in Informatics, Moscow : All-Union Institute for Scientific and Technological Information, 1969, pp. 120-142.
43. Bhattacharya, G., Information Sciences : A Unified View Through a Systems Approach, IASLIC, 1978, pp. 18-20.
44. *Ibid.,* p. 21.
45. Voigt, Melvin J., Scientists Approach to Information, New York : American Library Association, 1961 (ACRL, Monograph No. 24).
46. Nanun, Burt., *op.cit.,* p. 56.
47. McCarthy, J., Information, *op.cit.,* p.1.
48. Drucker, P.F., *op.cit.,* p. 27.
49. Wiener, N., The Human Use of Human Beings : Cybernetics and Society, 2nd ed. Garden City, New York : Doubleday and Company, 1954, p. 17, 39.
50. Rathswol, Engene J., Nature of Information, *In :* Perspectives in Information Science, *op.cit.,* pp. 21-24.

CHAPTER 3

INFORMATION GENERATION AND THE INFLUENCING FACTOR

Information Generation

Information generation is a continuous process. Information is like other commercial products which are produced and consumed by the society for its survival. There is great impact of two World Wars on the development of various fields of knowledge. "Information is needed to tell us what our society is like now, how rapidly and in what way it is changing, and what scientific and technical alternatives to present practices exist or can be found. Ideally, society should have mechanisms to ensure that decision-makers, including the public, have access to the information they need to determine what relations exist between current actions and future effects, to weigh the merits of alternative priority systems, to derive practical achievable goals for society and plan for the optimum allocation of finite resources to attain these goals."[1]

Information, in the published form of articles, books, monographs, etc., or in the form of data, is considered as resource and also serves as stimulus for the generation of new information. The information thus generated is the cause and cure of the problems. This shows that there is a link between society, man, his needs and information generation.

Advancements in the field of communication net-work have

brought down the distance between the persons, states, countries and continents throughout the world. Actually, the need for creative achievement has never been more recognised and desired than today.

Creative contributions are born when an individual is not content with the little known material and forces of nature, or man himself. Advances are given impetus when individuals feel compelled to fully develop and exercise their talents. We will continue to be confronted with competitive forces leading to creations as long as one person strives to advance, as long as one business attempts to increase its share of the total industrial output or to improve its profitability, or as long as one nation attempts to improve its world position.[2]

A person may have the most brilliant thoughts but until he brings them into the open where they can be of use to others, he has not created anything. The man who gives us a hare brained idea that could give us a lot of trouble and cost us a lot of money certainly would not be called creative. It implies that our ideas which have values would only be counted as creations. At the same time they should suit the problems and time of the society.

Information Creation

The art of creativity is confined relatively to a very small proportion of world's population, who could device new methods, reorganise existing ideas and offer improved solutions to the familiar problems. Mohsin (1963) in his Presidential address to the Eight All-India Guidance Conference held at Allahabad in 1963, expressed that "society consists of individuals. But it is only few exceptionally talented individuals who contribute most to the growth of the society. They create new horizons and set new standards in science, technology, literature, fine arts, business, industry and social leadership. No sooner does society become devoid of nature's gift of talent than it would start to stagnate and ultimately perish."[3]

Human beings are endowed with unique power of thinking and creation. Computer which can work with amazing feat cannot match the man, as it can only repeat the mechanical orientations but cannot produce original ideas which the human mind is capable of doing like that work of creation.

Necessary care is required in defining the term 'creativity', borrowed from religion, literature and science. It cannot be put in a single definition. Different thinkers viewed it from different perspectives.

According to Yamamoto (1964)[4] creativity is the process of forming new ideas of hypotheses, testing these ideas or hypotheses and communicating the results.

Foskett (1983)[5] states that creativity in art or in science consists in the ability to present information in a light which has not appeared before but which nevertheless adds to a coherent pattern already publicly available.

Rawlinson (1981)[6] says that creativity involves the relating of things or ideas which were previously unrelated.

Beveridge (1980)[7] views creativity as perceiving significantly new patterns in bits of knowledge—data and theories—already available.

According to E.de.Bono (1970)[8] the essence of creativity in problem-solving is the ability to break through constraints imposed by habit and tradition, so as to find 'new' solution to problems.

Whereas Parker (1963)[9] describes creativity as the art of seeking out, trying out and combining knowledge in new ways.

Mednick (1962)[10] also says that creativity involves the ability to make new combinations which have social worth.

In the opinion of Mackinnon (1960)[11] creativity is a process which has a time dimension, and which involves originality, adaptiveness and realization. According to him creativity is a long process comprising (*a*) a period of preparation during which a problem is selected; (*b*) a period of concentrated effort to solve the problem; (*c*) a period of withdrawal from the problem, i.e., a period of renunciation of the problem or recession from it; (*d*) a period of insight accompanied by the exhibition, glow, and elation of the 'aha' experience; and (*e*) a period of verification, evaluation and elaboration of the insight which one has experienced.

From these definitions it is evident that creativity is the product of human thinking, aiming at bringing out new information in bits or in the form of new solutions to problems or combining knowledge in new ways. A relation between the human mind or thinking and processing of data aimed at solving some problem is also seen in information generation. Thus, creativity and information generation have the common factors associated in process. In the process of creativity and information generation, we see new bits of knowledge —data and combining them in new ways, which have social worth. If something is to be called a creation or information, it must be useful and beneficial to mankind.

Growth of knowledge, whether we call it generation of new information, or creativity, or invention, or innovation, is a never ending process. All these are synonymous to the basic concept of research activity. As such, in this study creativity is taken to mean information creation.

Modes of Information Generation

Information generation involves the relating of ideas to originate new things to solve the problems. Further splitting or churning of the existing knowledge, viz., specializations and deep studies also lead to the generation of information.

J.H. Shera (1972)[12] identifies six kinds of information generation by various modes and they are as follow :

(*i*) **Conceptual information** — The ideas, theories, hypothese about the relationships which exist among the variables in the area of a problem.

(*ii*) **Empirical information** — Experience, the data of research may be drawn from one's self or through communication from others. It may be laboratory generated, or it may be product of the "Literature Search".

(*iii*) **Procedural information** — The methodology which enables the investigator to operate more effectively. Procedural information relates to the means by which the data of the investigation are obtained, manipulated and tested; it is essentially methodological and from it has been derived the "Scientific Attitude". The communication of procedural information from one discipline or field of investigation to another may illuminate vast shadows of human ignorance.

(*iv*) **Stimulatory information** — Man must be motivated and there are two sources for such motivation himself and his environment. Stimulatory information, that is environmentally derived, is probably most effective when it is transmitted by direct communication—the contagious enthusiasm of another individual—but whether directly or indirectly communicated it is probably the most difficult of all forms of information to systematise. It is by nature fortuitous; it submits unwillingly to direction or compulsion.

The growing emphasis on 'team' research derives from the natural gregariousness of man and his inherent propensity for group organisation and has been stimulated by the growing magnitude of the research task itself. The body of accumulated knowledge has assumed vast proportions and its mastery has become so highly specialised, that an increasing number of research undertakings require the concerted attack of many minds, with varying skills, aptitudes, experience and points of view. Team research magnifies and complicates the informational task and greatly increases its importance. To the four types of information listed, team research adds :

(*v*) **Policy information** — This is the source of the decision making process. Collective activity necessitates the definition and objective and purpose, the fixing of responsibility, the codification of rights and privileges and the delineation of function.

(*vi*) **Directive information** — Group activity cannot proceed effectively without coordination and it is through directive information that this coordination is achieved.

David Bawden (1986)[13] expresses that there are specific aspects related to scientific creativity, viz.

(*a*) the role of chance in discovery,

(*b*) the great value of analogies,

(*c*) the importance of careful examination of exceptions to, and inconsistencies within the accepted scheme of things,

(*d*) the damaging effect of commonly-held ideas which are in fact false, and

(*e*) the importance of inter-disciplinary research.

(a) Chance

"An information service can at times become itself a stimulus to creativity by providing a user with what is pertinent even though it may seem irrelevant. Chance favours the prepared mind and such serendipitous information is often the sort that leads to scientific revolutions."[14]

There are numerous instances in the scientific world, where chance observations have led to the discoveries and inventions by the great scientists. Examples, are 'Gravitational Force' discovered by Newton and 'Discovery of America' by Colombus. It happens in music also when new 'notes' are found by chance. So also in social sciences, where we come across new things of interest in literature while searching for an entirely different thing.

J.H. Austin (1978)[15] distinguishes four kinds of chance relevant to scientific creativity

Chance 1 : 'Blind luck', unattributable to any actions or qualitie of the recipient.

Chance 2 : 'Happy accidents', when unconnected events impinge upon the matter in hand. Favoured by exposure to seemingly unconnected facts and experiences.

Chance 3 : 'Prepared mind', 'Pasteur Principle'. New relationships are perceived because of exposure to many facts related to the problem in hand.

Chance 4 : Chance favouring the particular individual, because of distinctive knowledge, interests or lifestyle, seemingly far removed from the problem at hand.

(b) Analogies

Reasoning by an analogy plays an important part in scientific thought. An analogy can be brought between the fundamental categories of classification theory of Dr. Ranganathan.

It is said that "Ranganathan has derived the initial concept of his classification after seeing a demonstration of a toy erector set in Selfridge's Department Store."[16] Further Dr. Ranganathan takes the analogy of origin of the river Ganga from the Ramayana for comparing the life of a classification scheme. "The King Bhagiratha goes in advance in his chariot carving a suitable course for the river Ganga and the river it tamed and trained to follow that course. Similar is the relation between universe of subjects, theory of classification and scheme for classification."[17]

(c) Careful Study of Exceptions and Gaps

"The creative writer looks for flaws in the paradigm, for gaps and inconsistencies in our general picture of reality."[18] Now-a-days researchers are concentrating more on the gaps and lapses in the research works of their predecessors. This inquisitiveness is leading to the generation of new information. For this, researchers use the libraries and their services to find and to look and think deeply into the observations seeming at complete variance with the existing ideas. Here also chance plays a good role.

(d) False Knowledge

Scientists say that there is great danger of false information in the literature, presenting a barrier to new ideas. We should not forget that out-dated knowledge is otherwise false. So the ability forget the past ideas and habits has been held to be one of the most important aspects of innovation.

(e) Interdisciplinary Research

Interdisciplinary research has gained good momentum and importance in the modern world. Scientists have emphasised the need for inter-disciplinary contacts. The benefit of the cross fertilization and the fact that the best side for the generation of new ideas is the interface of two scientific disciplines. It is assumed that research in pure disciplines, even though making great advances in the field, if not useful for everyday life, is a waste. Under inter-disciplinary research, here we can take the example of library user studies, which are related with the psychology of the persons. Mathematics and Psychology are the disciplines which are frequently interlinked with other disciplines of both sciences and non-sciences in research works.

Creativity Stimulation Techniques

Bawden (1986)[19] summarises the techniques that stimulate creativity as follows :

(*i*) **Synectics** — Defined as the joining together of different and apparently irrelevant elements to solve a problem. Synectics is based on the use of analogical thinking, to seek similarities between apparently different things. Very far from obvious links are deliberately sought, in order to test assumptions about possible solutions. Applications of the technique may require the involvement of specialists in fields far removed from the problem under investigation.

(*ii*) **Brain Storming** — In this procedure check lists which have relevance to solve a problem are prepared. From this, unconventional ideas are sought and the brain storming technique relegates evaluation and criticism of the ideas produced to a later stage and encourage freedom in generating new concepts.

(*iii*) **Morphological Analysis** — In this technique all information potentially relevant to the solution of a problem is systematically examined. Available information is grouped into 'attributes' of concepts or things all and combinations are examined. Illogical combinations also are tried for feasible alternatives to solve the problems. The process of morphological analysis being exhaustive, reduces the risk of novel combinations being overlooked. The systematic and objective synthesis of possible solutions avoids the constraints of pre-conceived ideas.

(*iv*) **Lateral Thinking** — Here, number of techniques are used for restructuring conceptual patterns and creating new ones, essentially looking at familiar data in new ways. Irrelevant information is also sought to work out suitable correct solutions. In this technique random stimulation is largely used. This may include exposure to ideas from a completely different field, by totally cross-disciplinary discussions, or by entirely random browsing in a library. De Bono suggests the 'formal' introduction of randomness by random selection of an article from a book or journal, or a word from a dictionary as a stimulus to problem-solving. Alternatively different aspects or relevant material are used as alternative entry points to begin problem-solving.

Through the brief survey of some aspects of scientific creativity and creativity stimulation techniques, Bawden (1986)[20] has identified a number of points clearly related to information provision, listed in Table 3.1.

Table 3.1
Some Aspects of Information Handling to Aid Creativity

S.No	Aspects
1.	Recognising/creating patterns
2.	Identifying analogies
3.	Interdisciplinary contact
4.	Dealing with false knowledge
5.	Identifying exceptions/inconsistencies
6.	Favouring chance
7.	Random stimulation of ideas
8.	Temporary suspension of evaluation

Source : Bawden, David, 1986.

Bawden says that in creativity some aspects are related to the sort of information provided (e.g., inter-disciplinary), the way in which it is provided (e.g., to identify analogies), and the way in which it is handled (e.g., temporary acceptance of false information).[21]

Occasions Leading to Information Generation by the University Teachers

Occasions are the stimulations for new ideas. The spark of a new idea as a base leads to information generation. Among University teachers, keeping in view their working situations, the following occasions can be accounted, where the teacher gets inspired by new ideas for generating information.

(*i*) **Class-room Work** — Teachers are primarily involved in teaching activity. To keep the students abreast of the latest developments through their lectures, they generally read more and more to gather information about the trends in the development of the subject. On such occasions some new ideas flash in mind, which become the base for information generation.

(*ii*) **Zeal to Participate in Seminars and Conferences** — The zeal to participate in seminars and conferences never keeps the active teacher idle. He or she will be always keeping open the eye for new ideas. This kind of vigorous thinking churns the existing knowledge and the personal experiences and gives birth to new concepts.

(*iii*) **Discussions** — Discussions with professional colleagues, friends and peers in the subject fields and even with family members are the occasions, where a teacher gets new ideas and plans for generating information.

(*iv*) **Promotional Opportunities** — Selections and promotions to higher cadres based on merit are other occasions for generating information in the form of publications and guiding research works leading to M. Phils and Ph. Ds. Thus, this factor is motivating the university teachers who aspire promotion to higher cadres to generate more information.

The present study is, however, confined to the following inspiring sources that lead to information generation among university academicians :

(*a*) Discussion with family members,

(*b*) Discussion with friends other than professional colleagues,

(*c*) Discussion with professional colleagues,

(*d*) While participating in conferences/seminars, etc.,

(*e*) While reading a book,

(*f*) While contemplating on an article, and

(*g*) When sitting alone and thinking.

The analysed data pertaining to this part is presented in the analysis part of the present study.

Mere inspiration cannot make a person generate new information. The surroundings in which he lives and works influence the act of information generation. Thus, the influencing factors have become the part of the cycle of information generation.

Factors Influencing Generation of Information

Information is generated when an individual is not satisfied with the little he knows about the materials, the nature and the man himself. The spirit of competition is leading to creations in all fields viz., business, industry, science and technology, as long as the persons strive to advance. This kind of personal efforts are strengthening the position of the country in the world. Struggle for existence is the basic motivation for the man to create new things or improve such things to overcome the problem.

It is a known fact that where there is no vision, the people will perish. The social and economic problems are forcing the learned community to find out the remedies, by way of research. Need is the mother of invention. The social needs of man made the researcher to invent new equipments, new varieties of seeds in the field of agriculture, new medicines for varieties of diseases, etc. As a whole, needs of man made him change the social standards of the present day.

The research activities thus, are not confined to the globe. Further studies are in progress on the planets and satellites to find their suitability for living and other purposes of the human beings. At each and every stage of these research activities, new information is generated.

Scientists, Engineers, Managers and Teachers are among those, who are involved in the generation of new information. The scientist continues to browse through the literature throughout his research activity, to stimulate lines of thought process. This habit of reading is compulsory, which helps him acquaint with the developments in his subject area of interest. Even to get specific data and information needed at different stages of his research work, the researcher is supposed to read and read then bring out the results and build up the gap between the research outcomes of previous years or bring new things to the light.

According to Viswanathan (1976), "the fundamental aim and function of research is to find solutions to problems confronted in the course of human activity in a variety of situations and in the midst of available data on accomplished work and output. Questions are raised and answers are found, but the quality and quantity of answers to these problems are new information generation. This seems to be an unending cycle, because the human mind is as restless as the restless atom, always on the forward march, engaged in ceaseless thinking and producing a prolific output of information."[22]

Influence of National and International Situations on Research Activities

According to Kurt Sontheimer (1971), "the modern trend towards research into the future purports to be quite different from previous approaches to prediction. Those involved consider their work to be

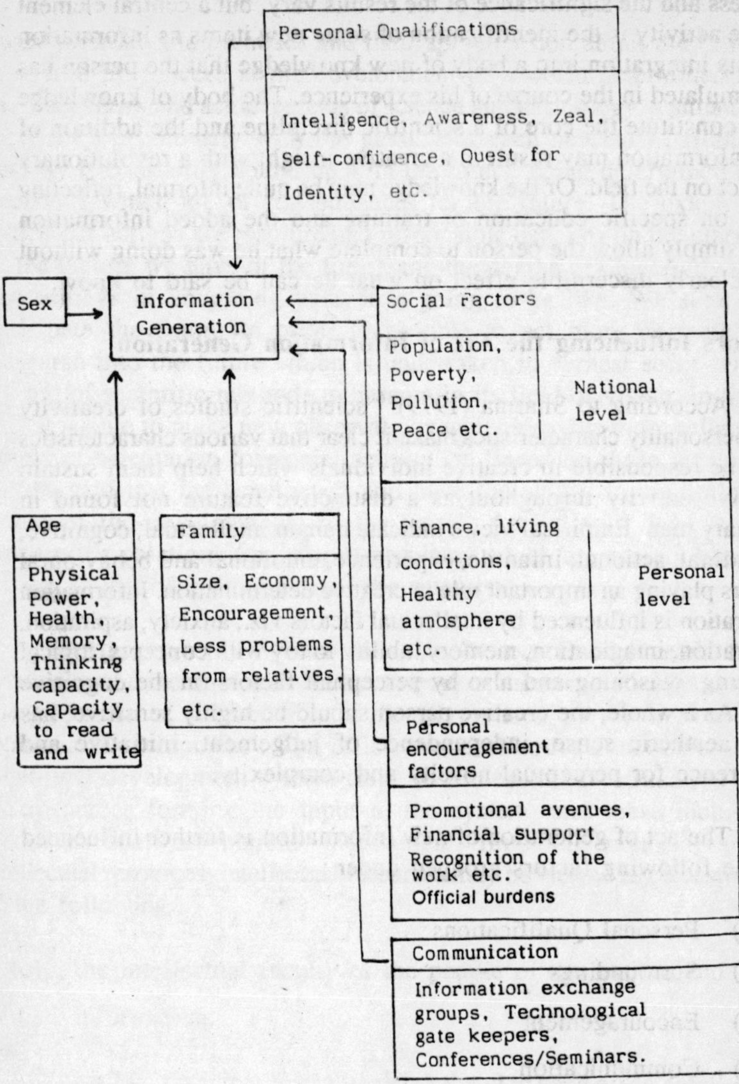

Fig. 3.1

Factors Influencing Information Generation

Personal Qualifications

Nobel Prize Winner Prof. H.C. Adolf Butenandt says that "it (research) is a human activity undertaken in a systematic and rationally verifiable manner and directed towards the acquiring of new knowledge. In order to pursue such activity the individual has to possess certain personal qualifications which can be developed and strengthened as the scientific activity proceeds. The researcher has to possess a certain amount of daring if he is to devote a part of his life to a task in which he cannot be sure from the outset that he will achieve his goal. One requires independence of character or faith in one's own abilities if one is to go beyond the frame-work of seemingly established knowledge and, whether by means of experiment or through theoretical deliberation, to establish safe new paths into previously unknown regions. One needs to check the accuracy of existing sets of facts and existing theories and at the same time constantly to subject the results of one's own deliberations and work to the criticism of others. One has to be willing to defend one's own point of view in discussion with others, and listen to and accept other peoples arguments if they are convincing. One has to be aware that there are limits to our knowledge and one has to respect the works of the creation, for which those of us who use our intellect also have to bear responsibility. One has to experience and register the miraculous nature of those works and to inquire into the purpose of existence."[27]

A creative scientist should be alert to his surroundings in sensing the future. He must be active in completing his aims and objectives even by sacrificing the things for this purpose. Interest in solving the complex problems is the basic essence of the act of creativity. Roe (1951)[28], through her 'psychological study on physical scientists' has observed among the scientists, lack of personal love, self-discipline, motivation, non-social movements and less maturity on sex as the basic characteristics that made them generate more information by concentrating on research activities. She has further found independence and self-sufficiency as distinctive characteristics among the persons involved in scientific creativity.

Further, Mac Kinnon (1962)[29] found creative scientists more independent of thought and action, freedom from conventional restraints and strong achievement motivation in independently judging situations.

Through the Conference Paper submitted by Mac Kinnon (1963)[30] at the Institute of Personality Assessment and Measurement (IPAR) at the University of California, it is noted that creative persons are intelligent, original, independent in thought and action, open to experience both of the inner self and the outer world, intutive, aesthetically sensitive and free from crippling restraints. They have high energy level, a persistent commitment to creative endeavour and a strong sense of destiny which includes a degree of resoluteness and a measure of egotism.

Eiduson (1962) differentiated the following personality characteristics of creative scientists from that of non-creative scientists; they remain interested in complex intellectual deeds, emotional in intellectual works, independent of emotional behaviour, sensitive towards others and themselves, unconventional, original, receptive about his internal needs and wishes, ability to express his experiences, more ego involved in their works and struggle with them.[31]

Cattell and Drevdhal (1955)[32] in their comparative study on Personality Profiles found the scientist quite different from the average people in so many aspects. They found the scientist highly intelligent, independent of mind, i.e., free thinking, dominant by nature, sensitive towards surroundings, reserved and cool, inhibited, serious and self confident.

George F. Kneller (1965)[33] has elaborately dealt with the personality characteristics of creative persons touching such traits as intelligence, awareness, fluency, flexibility and originality, elaboration, skepticism, persistence, humour and self-confidence.

Foster (1971) reports that "the characteristics of the creative personality are probably many and varied but such attributes as sensitivity, tender-mindedness, emotional stability and an ability to remain uncommitted and receptive to experiences seem to be important."[34]

Barron (1963) finds the creative persons more comfortable with disorder and more challenged to find a subtle way of recording. He is more independent of judgement, more troubled about the world and has more resources for dealing with his troubles.[35]

According to Von Fange (1964)[36] characteristics such as habits, functional fixedness, individual reactions and unsympathetic environment affect the act of creativity. Creative workers have devised many techniques through the years to aid themselves in overcoming their habits and stiff attitudes.

According to Freud (1959)[37] a happy person never fantasises, only an unsatisfied one does. The motive forces of fantasis are unsatisfied wishes and every single fantasy is the fulfilment of a wish, a correction of unsatisfying reality. These motivating wishes vary according to sex, character and circumstances of the person who is having fantasy, but they fall naturally into two main groups. They are either ambitious wishes, which serve to elevate the subject's personality or they are erotic ones.

David Krech (1970), expresses that "the creative mind is an active mind, constantly questioning. A necessary condition for the creative experience is intellectual independence ... ideas arise and solutions to problems emerge from within, often in a spontaneous, enigmatic and mysterious fashion ... Collaboration with others appears to some as a significant source of a stimulation. The opportunity to exchange views with members of other disciplines is also considered productive."[38]

According to Kochen (1969), "the active contributors can be modelled as information processors for: (1) question-asking, or recognizing what is known to be unknown in a field, (2) question-answering or puzzle-solving; (3) fact-finding; (4) applications; and most important, (5) theory formation. As such they interact not only with each other and documents, but with the paradigm characterizing the field."[39]

Social Factors

The interaction between human beings and their environment initiates the individual for certain creative activities. Naturally, knowledge grows in the individuals by learning process. Reading makes the man perfect his way of thinking. Reading of books, journals, etc., makes him come close to the society and its problems and needs, which make him understand his surroundings where he lives. This alerts the mind of a creative person to think of solutions or find out remedies, which naturally lead to scientific advancement and revolution.

Khanna accounts the following social factors that lead to the knowledge explosion[40]:

The increase in population pressure and the rise in the standard of living;population pressure has gone beyond the capacity of natural and near natural commodities to maintain the people. The result of this is the intensification of production of natural commodities and production of artificial commodities.

To satisfy the material wants such as food, clothing, housing facilities and transport facilities, requires continuous research on large scale viz., developmental research, pragmatic research, applied research and pure or fundamental research.

The social pressure demands that the interval between any major invention or discovery and its exploitation for human purposes should be reduced towards a vanishing point.

Population pressure as the chief factor is forcing the learned community to find out the devices to control it and also to meet the needs of the growing population. In Medical Science after research, methods of controlling the birth rate have been found viz., family planning operations, condoms, etc. So many kinds of medicines, for various diseases that we are seeing in the market today are the outcome of research of great scientists, who have taken up their work keeping in view the prosperity of the society. On the same lines, to meet the needs of food-grains for the growing population a variety of hybrid crops are found out by way of research by the agricultural scientists. The concept of economy is playing a great role in the society. So developing countries within the available meagre financial sources plan for the growth of science and technology that serves the social needs of the country. The outcome of this multi-purpose projects, developments in mechanical engineering, electrical and electronics engineering, etc.

Sound economy and social freedom are also found influencing the act of information generation. Independent thinkers are able to function effectively when they are emotionally and socially free. This can be observed by comparing social conditions among developed and developing countries with regard to the rapidity in research activities. Because of this economy and social freedom, USA, USSR, Japan, Britain and other developed countries are at the top in all fields of developments viz., medicine, engineering, agriculture, defence science, space science, etc.

Mackinnon (1963) gives paramount importance to environmental conditions, needs and goals as the main factors that affect and control the act of creativity. A scientist acts as a mediator between externally defined needs and goals. Environment plays a key role for the production of a novel or appropriate product, which is not related to the inner state of the scientist. This type of creative products are generally found in the research works of scientists, engineers, chemists, biologists and technologists.[41] Von Fange (1964) expresses that "our emotions and the attitudes present in environment in our surroundings and in ourselves can stimulate us to great creative achievements. They can more easily impede or stop our advances."[42]

Pollution and Peace are the other social factors influencing the generation of new knowledge. The creative person wishes his surroundings to be peaceful and unpolluted. The calm atmosphere allows them to concentrate more on their work, by way of thinking. Researchers enjoy more in reading documents in the calm atmosphere. Pollution here includes noise, air and even the troublesome neighbours. Sometimes it so happens that creative persons are disturbed by the nasty behaviour of their neighbours at home and their colleagues in the institutions. Hence, healthy atmosphere in the surroundings plays a prominent role in the life of a scientist, engineer, manager, teacher, etc., who is involved in research activity.

Personal Encouragement Factors

Some methods have been adopted to encourage the research activity among scientists and creativity among writers. The fulfilment of personal requirements and ambitions of the information generators is inevitable where they can use their brain for the development of the nation. Motivation in one form or the other accelerates the research activity of the person. The following are some of the motivating factors for academic communities.

(*a*) Promotional Avenues,

(*b*) Financial Assistance,

(*c*) Recognition of the Research Work,

(*d*) Encouragement from Colleagues Friends, and

(*e*) Team Research Spirit.

There are chances of creativity being hampered with the official burdens. It is true with professional jobs viz., doctors, engineers, teachers and managers. In all these cases the day-to-day official duties are to be discharged in the way of creativity. Non-peaceful life, insufficient time to sit and think and the mechanised life are the closely related obstacles. The attitude of the higher officials, friends and colleagues plays a key role on the psychology of the creative person. Encouragement from these circles inspire him to take up more and more research work, leading to generation of new information.

Communication

International, national and regional conferences or meetings play an important role as the media in the communication of information. These are the places where discussions between the participants take place. These discussions may be among large groups, small groups or between the individuals. The exchange of thoughts, help the participants either giving rise to new ideas or getting feed-back or both.

Invisible college groups, which comprise prominent and respected researchers, who are acquainted with each other and communicate with each other, are the high producers in terms of number of papers. The communication between the members of the group is crucial and at the forefront of the research area.[43]

According to Meadows, an increase in the number of contacts a scientist has, naturally increases the extent to which he carries out his research work in collaboration with others. It is hardly surprising, therefore, that the more productive scientists also tend to publish more joint papers. In universities, the greater the extent to which members of a department involve themselves in extra departmental communication, the greater is their productivity. Further, in universities, higher productivity results because of wider contacts between the scientists. The larger the research group to which a scientist belongs the higher the productivity is likely to be seen.[44]

Meadows says that, "communication in one form or the other usually takes up a significant fraction of a scientist's working life".[45] H. Menzel et. al., (1960) studied the time spent by the US Chemists on scientific communication. According to their report, university chemists spent nearly quarter of their working day in scientific communication, while chemists in industrial organizations spent almost a third of thier time in this way. The University chemists divided their time equally betwen receiving and giving information, whereas the industrial chemists spent two-thirds of their time receiving.[46] Hence, the difference in information generation between the university teacher scientist and the industrial scientist.

Family

David Krech (1970) says that "rigidity and becoming set in a particular thought pattern stand in the way of the creative process. Such factors as being too concerned about the future, concerned about failure or preoccupied with problems of every day reality can also generate one's productivity. All these seem to work against the kind of open mindedness required."[47] Family background plays a key-role on the life style of a man. "Often the mother is recalled as a great source of encouragement, and some feel their mother were significant in their careers. The impact of an older or younger brother as a source of inspiration or a colleague is seen in a number of instances."[48] The other factors that are accountable being meeting deadlines, the need to get a job, to earn more and more money, etc.

The size of the family, the attitude of the mother, wife and children; the burdens such as education of the children, marriages of the dependents; health problems of the family members as well as personal problems with the relatives and with neighbours are the paramount factors linked with the act of information generation.

Age

Age and sex are also influencing the research activity of the scientist. The information generation is constantly growing with age or there is decline in it. There are studies relating to creative characteristics of persons at different ages. Rossman (1935) made a study of the childhood, education and age of 710 Inventors. The result showed that inventions started in the early years of adulthood of the inventors, than creative persons of other fields. Rossman observed that 61 percent made their inventions before they attained the age of twenty years, averaging 21-23 years of age.[49]

Lehman (1953)[50] says that age is not the only factor that affects information generation but there are other factors such as decline in physical power, sensory and motor capacities, serious illness or bodily infirmities, glandular changes, material and sexual problems, death of a loved one, preoccupation with practical demands of life, responsibilities, desiring prestige than creativity, contentment due to early creations, apathy due to non-recognition, negative transfer, decreased motivation, psychotic tendency and dėvelopment of alcoholism or narcotism. Through his study he found that position, field, income and other factors control the act of creativity. According to him, chemists contribute to the growth of knowledge most between 26 and 30 years of age, the mathematicians between 30 and 40; musicians between 30 and 40; authors under 45; and philosophers between 35 and 39. He viewed that creativity is peak at the age of thirties and then declines slowly.

Dennis (1954)[51] had made a critical and elaborate study on the change in productivity with age among the psychologists born in mid-nineteenth century. The outcome of the study was that the creativity was the same throughout all the ages. High producers used to produce more and more, whereas the low producers remained as low producers. A comparison of this data was made with the data drawn from the membership of the National Academy of Science (Table 3.2).[52]

Table 3.2
Average Productivity Per Decade of Life

Decade of Life	20-30	30-40	40-50	50-60	60-70
Psychologists	1.5	7.4	11.4	11.7	11.7
Members of N.S.A.	15.0	48.4	47.1	47.3	36.6

Source : Meadows, A.J., 1974.

The results of the comparison between psychologists and academy scientists showed the increase in information creation in the later case, correspondingly with age. At the age of seventy, the publications were as high as 765 in number and as minimum as 27. Whereas among psychologists at the age of seventy the productivity was as high as 240 publications the minimum of 2. However, when the increase in productivity was compared from decade to decade of life, proved to be small in both the cases. There is no sign of productivity peaks in the span, which normally depend on circumstances.

According to Smith and Kragh (1975)[53] creative process in adults differs from creative process in adolescents and also in children. Creativity at a mature age is primarily associated with recreation of dormant developmental alternatives once discarded in favour of the main line of development; and in principle, the normal adult need not lack creative possibilities. Creative efforts in middle age are however, affected by social factors in addition to the physical fitness, i.e., thinking capacity, retaining the thought contents in memory, capacity to read and write, etc.

Sex

Now-a-days sex is the neglected factor that can be related with creativity in the society. Females are competing with males in every field and moving together to share the social responsibilities. Both the sexes are doing research works aimed at the uplift of the society in the fields of science and technology and social and behavioural sciences.

According to Cole and Cole (1973)[54] and Kyvik (1950)[55] males are found more productive than females, publishing an average 40-50 percent more papers than their female counterparts. The study of Palmer (1991)[56] also revealed that a group of scientists containing 50 percent female showed a slightly lower publishing rate than other groups which contained 11 to 15 percent female scientists.

However, till recently in India woman was more confined to the affairs of the family. Generally, she concentrates on the welfare of the children and other members of the family. Although, she equally bears the burdens of the family, social-freedom is less seen among Indian women compared with the women of the Western countries. This automatically makes them less aware of the social problems and affects free thinking.

Raina (1971)[57] conducted tests to find out the influence of sex on teachers with regard to imagination and verbal and non-verbal creative thinking. He observed that sex has no impact. Prior to this, McElvian and others (1963)[58] who have studied 209 teachers from the Eastern Washington State College concluded that sex does not play any part on creativity. Alpaugh and Birren (1975)[59] through their studies on young, middle aged and older people, found that the degree of sex role is not significantly related to creativity.

Scientists from the Western countries have studied the influence of qualitative factors viz., intelligence, dynamism, fluency, originality, self-confidence, etc., on the act of creativity. In this study only the quantitative factors are studied in relation to their impact on information generation by the university teachers. These factors are grouped into helpful factors as unhelpful factors as shown below :

Helpful factors for information generation are :

(*a*) Faculty Environment,

(*b*) Recognition of the Work, and

(*c*) Financial Assistance.

Unhelpful factors for information generation are :

(*a*) Domestic Factors viz., family size and burdens, health problems, problems from relatives and neighbours, etc.; and

(*b*) Academic and Official Factors viz., Headship, Chairmanship of Board of Studies, teaching activity, research guidance, problems from friends and officials, etc.

The analysed data pertaining to this aspect is presented in the analysis part of this study.

REFERENCES

1. Artandi, Susan., Man, Information and Society—New Patterns of Interaction, *Journal of the American Society for Information Science*, January 1979, p. 15.
2. Von Fange, Eugene K., Professional Creativity, Englewood Cliffs, N.J.: Prentice Hall, 1964, p. 2.
3. Eighth All-India Guidance Conference, Allahabad, 1963, Presidential Address of Mohsin, p. 152.
4. Yamamoto, K., Creative Thinking—Some Thoughts on Research. *Exceptional Children*, 30, 1964, pp. 403-410.
5. Foskett, D.J., Pathways for Communication, London : Bingley, 1983, p. 42.
6. Rawlinson, J.G., Creative Thinking and Brain-storming, London : Gower, 1981.
7. Beveridge, W.I.B., Seeds of Discovery, London : Heinemann, 1980.
8. de Bono, E., Lateral Thinking —A Textbook of Creativity, London, Ward Lock, 1970.
9. Parker, D.H., Schooling for Individual Excellence, London : Nelson, 1963.
10. Mednick, S.A., The Association Concept of the Creative Process, *Psychological Reviews*, 69, 1962, pp. 220-232.
11. Mackinnon, D.W., What Do You Mean by Talent and How Do We Test For It ? The Search for Talent, New York : College Entrance Board, 1960, pp. 20-29.
12. Shera, J.H., The Foundations of Education for Librarianship, New York : Becker and Hayes, 1972, p. 175.
13. Bawden, David., Information Systems and the Stimulation of Creativity, *Journal of Information Science*, 12, 1986, pp. 205-206.

14. Foskett, D.J., *op.cit.*, p. 83.
15. Austin, J.H., Chase, Chance and Creativity, Columbia : Columbia University Press, 1978.
16. Garfield, E., A Tribute to Ranganathan, *Current Contents*, 6, 1984, pp. 3-10.
17. Ranganathan, S.R., Colon Classification, Ed. 7: A Preview., Sarada Ranganathan Endowment, Bangalore : DRTC, 1969, p. 21.
18. Foskett, D.J., *op.cit.*, p. 51.
19. Bawden, David., *op.cit.*, pp.206-207.
20. *Ibid.*, p. 207.
21. *Ibid.*, p. 207.
22. Viswanathan, C.G., Elements of Information Science, New Delhi : Today and Tomorrow, 1976, p. 11.
23. Sontheimer, Kurt., Prediction as the Aim and Problem of Modern Social Science, *Universitas,* 14(1), 1971, p. 2.
24. Bhattacharya, G., Information Science : A Unified View Through A System—Approach., IASLIC, 1978, pp. 22-23.
25. Walker, Donald E., The Organization and Use of Information : Contributions of Information Science, Computational Linguistics and Artificial Intelligence, *Journal of American Society for Information Science,* 32(5), 1981, p. 347.
26. Sharma, K.N., Dynamics of Creativity, Agra : National Psychological Corporation, 1979, p. 4.
27. Adolf Butenandt, H.C., The Role of Research and the Problems Involved in Promoting It. *Universitas,* 15(1), 1973, p.6.
28. Roe, Anne., A Psychological Study on Physical Scientists., *Psychological Monograph,* 43, 1951, pp. 121-239.
29. Mac Kinnon, D.W., The Nature and Nature of Creative Talent, *American Psychologist,* 17(7), 1962, pp. 484-495.
30 Mac Kinnon, D.W., Personality Correlates of Creativity, a paper presented at the Second Conference on Thinking, National Education Association, Washington, 2-4 May, 1963.
31. Eiduson, B.T., Scientists-Their Psychological World. New York : Basic Books, 1962.
32. Cattell, R.B. and Drevdahl, J.E.A., A Comparison of the Personality Profile (16 PF) of Eminent Researchers with that of Eminent Teacher and Administrators and of the General Population, *British Journal of Psychology,* 46, 1955, pp. 248-61.
33. Kneller, George, F., The Art and Science of Creativity, New York : Rinehart and Winston, Inc., 1965.
34. Foster, John, Creativity and the Teacher, London : Macmillan, 1971, p. 33.
35. Barron Frank., Creativity and Psychological Health, Cited in John Foster; *Ibid.*, pp. 26-27.
36. Von Fange, Eugene K., Professional Creativity, Englewood Cliffs, N.J. : Prentice Hall, 1964, p. 37.
37. Freud, Sigmund, Creative Writers and Day-dreaming, London : The Hogarth Press and The Institute of Psycho-analysis, 1959, Vol. 9, pp. 146-147.

38. Krech, David, Behavioural Science. *In :* Rosner, Stanley and Abt, Lawrence (Ed.) : The Creative Experience, New York : Grossman Publishers, 1970, pp. 383-384.
39. Kochen, Manfred, Stability in the Growth of Knowledge, *American Documentation,* 20(3), 1969, p. 191.
40. Khanna, J.K., Communicating Knowledge : Gateway to Knowledge, Kurukshetra : Research Publications, Vol. 1, pp. 8-11.
41. Mackinnon, D.W., Identifying and Developing Creativity, *Journal of Secondary Education,* 38, 1963, pp. 166-174.
42. Von Fange, Eugene, K., *Op.cit.,* p. 74.
43. De Solla Price, D.J., Little Science—Big Science, New York : Columbia University Press, 1963.
44. Meadows, A.J., Communication in Science, London : Butterworths, 1974, pp. 194-195.
45. *Ibid.,* p. 91.
46. Menzel, H., *et. al.,* Review of Studies in the Flow of Information Among Scientists, Vol.2, Columbia University, Bureau of Applied Social Research, 1960.
47. Krech, David, *op.cit.,* p. 385.
48. *Ibid.,* p.386.
49. Rossman, J., A Study of the Childhood, Education, and Age of 710 Inventors,. *Journal of Patent Office Society,* 17, 1935, pp. 411-421.
50. Lehman, H.C., Age and Achievement,. Princeton, N.J.: Princeton University Press, 1953.
51. Dennis, Wayne, Productivity Among American Psychologists, *American Psychologist,* 9, 1954, pp. 191-194.
52. Meadows, A.J., *op.cit.,* p. 187.
53. Smith, C.J. and Kragh, Ulf., Creativity in Mature and Old Age, *Psychological Research Bulletin,* 15(7), 1975, pp.1-17.
54. Cole, J.R. and Cole, S., Social Stratification in Science, Chicago : Chicago University Press, 1973.
55. Kyvik, S., Motherhood and Scientific Productivity, *Social Studies of Science,* 20, 1990, pp. 149-160.
56. Palmer, Judith., Scientists and Information : I. Using Cluster Analysis to Identify Information Style, *Journal of Documentation,* 47(2), 1991, p.116.
57. Raina, M.K., Verbal and Non-verbal Creative Thinking Ability—A Study in Sex Differences, *Journal of Education and Psychology,* 29(3), 1971, pp. 175-179.
58. McElvian, J.L. *et al.,* Relationship Between Creativity and Teacher Variability. *Psychological Reports,* 13, 1963.
59. Alpaugh, P.K. and Birren, Jame E., Are There Sex Differences in Creativity Across the Adult Life Span ? *Human Development,* 18(6), 1975, pp. 461-465.

CHAPTER 4

INFORMATION GENERATION AND ACADEMIC COMMUNITY

The strength of a country mainly lies in its resource, in its people and in the ability of those people to use and apply their resources efficiently and effectively. It is the University that produces great scientists, engineers, doctors, etc., who are directly involved in the growth of the nation and welfare of the society.

The modern university is a part of the real world, sharing its risks and responsibilities, its problems and obligations, its poverty and wealth. Hommadi (1984)[1] states that the goals of a university should be concerned with the research activities leading to the growth of new knowledge and communication of knowledge to enhance its value. He further adds that students should be trained in liberal arts and professions so that they can efficiently serve the society and solve the problems, viz. health, trade, agriculture, commerce, etc.

University—Its Goals

"The University is an institution designed for the advancement and dissemination of knowledge. The purpose of the University is to benefit the community and mankind in general through the advancement and dissemination of knowledge."[2] It is implied that the university has sub-systems—one for the dissemination of knowledge by way of teaching and second being the advancement of knowledge by way of research. The functions of both the sub-systems are aimed at solving the problems and meeting the needs of the society.

According to Hommadi (1984)[3] the University exists to serve a multiplicity of purposes. They are —

1. To preserve universe of knowledge and culture,
2. To transfer knowledge,
3. To introduce renovations and innovations in the universe of knowledge through pure and applied research,
4. To serve the society by solving the problems of health, transportation, law, trade, commerce, agriculture and industry etc.,
5. To encourage change,
6. To instruct and train students in liberal arts, professions and other forms of instruction,
7. To provide the students with every opportunity to develop the mind, strengthen the body, spark the imagination, control the emotions, strengthen the will and sharpen conscience, and
8. To provide a variety of student services such as feeding, housing, medical care, counselling and assistance in finding employment.

Kaysen (1969)4 identified the following four types of social functions of the higher education system :

1. Creation of new knowledge and its integration into the present body of knowledge in the widest sense;
2. To transmit the knowledge to the new general which has. two aspects —
   (*a*) transmission of general culture (i.e., education) and
   (*b*) transmission of the varieties of expert knowledge;
3. The application of knowledge to the solution of practical problems in the wider society; and

4. Socialization of late adolescents and young adults, teaching them how to fit into the social roles they will fill as adults.

Kerr (1963) states that "the university as producer, whole saler, and retailer of knowledge cannot escape service. Knowledge today is for everybody's sake."[5] According to Kerr, the post-war university has enormous growth, service oriented, meeting the needs of humans, multi-functional, composed of many and unrelated communities and its programmes are either influenced or determined by the social needs.

As such the objectives of the University should be aimed at social problems and needs and plan the academic and research activities to solve them.

Objectives and Functions of Universities in Indian Scene

"The objectives of an Indian University during pre-Independence period had been to strive to achieve the goals that were set by foreigners to promote their own interests. The earliest universities of modern India, i.e., Calcutta, Madras and Bombay, all founded in 1857, were established not for the advancement of learning and research but to conduct examinations and award degrees as a hallmark of fitness for recruitment to the civil service of the country."[6]

The functions of the universities after Independence in India have changed. Education Commission (1964-66), under the Chairmanship of D.S. Kothari, has listed the following functions to be performed by the Indian Universities —

1. "To seek and cultivate new knowledge, to engage vigorously and fearlessly in the pursuit of truth and to interpret old knowledge and beliefs in the light of new needs and discoveries;

2. To provide the right kind of leadership in all walks of life, to identify gifted youth and help them develop their potential to the full by cultivating physical fitness, developing the powers of the mind and cultivating right interests, attitudes and moral and intellecutal values;

3. To provide society with competent men and women trained in agriculture, arts, medicine, science and technology and various other professions who will also be cultivated individuals, imbued with a sense of social purpose;

4. To strive to promote equality and social justice and to reduce social and cultural differences through diffusion of education; and

5. To foster in the teachers and students, and through them in the society, generally, the attitudes and values needed for developing the good life in individuals and society."[7]

However, C.G. Viswanathan puts in simple terms the objectives and aims of the universities and other institutions of higher learning as —

1. "The conservation of knowledge and ideas;

2. Their transmission through teaching; and

3. Expansion of knowledge by research, publication, extension service and interpretation."[8]

Universities are involved with the activities of teaching and research and awarding of degrees after conducting examinations among the affiliated colleges. Vocational courses are also run by some universities, keeping in view the social needs and problems.

Consultancy and interaction of various departments of the university with industry and public bodies have proved beneficial to the development of the country. Universities should function like research institutes in exploring the natural sources and utilising them for the benefit of the society.

India being a developing country, the contributions of the Universities could be effectively used. The rich potential the Universities have, should be utilised properly and effectively. Then only the research and knowledge will prove useful to the nation.

University Teacher

The University teaching faculty comprises Professors, Readers, Lecturers and Demonstrators. The division of the cadres varies in some universities, where Associate Professors and Directors, Assistant Directors besides the above mentioned cadres are also seen. Huge buildings, well equipped laboratories, a library with good collection and the beautiful gardens and calm atmosphere are the assets among other requirements. All these are the accessories required for prosecuting and promoting higher education. "At the bottom, the quality of a university is always in direct proportion to the quality of its teachers."[9] So teachers are the basic pillars to the university, on whose shoulders the reputation of the university lies.

The teachers need to be constantly educated through refresher courses so that they can be effective in bringing about the desired changes, especially in the context of their changing roles in this fast changing dynamic society. They are not only expected to be thorough and upto date in their knowledge and comprehension of their chosen disciplines but also as facilitators or managers of learning are expected to be competent in the planning, organising, implementing, monitoring and evaluating the teaching learning process.[10]

Keeping in view the importance of the teacher, the selection committees of the universities used to search for well talented and learned persons. The common criteria for selection being eminence in a specialised field, ability to pursue independent research, and abiliy to inspire students with enthusiasm for study.[11]

According to Caston (1977) rewards and prestige will go to those teachers who distinguish themselves in research. Teaching is viewed as a less visible activity. Caston viewed education as the discipline for the adventure of life, research is intellectual adventure; and the universities should be homes of adventure shared in common by young and old.[12]

The Twentieth Century started with important differences in the English and American Universities. In England, the emphasis is given more on under-graduate teaching and development of the whole man, whereas in the United States importance is given to serious scholarship and research in the graduate schools. Possession of the Ph.D. is considered as a pre-requisite for teaching profession and at the same time it is viewed as a prestigious degree. This ultimately influences the graduates and diverts their activities towards research and specialization in their fields. Research projects—single handed or team research—have begun to gain momentum.

Because of these activities by the mid-Century of the post-World War period, the professor was less identified with the university than with the discipline. Hoffman (1970) states that the 'Knowledge Explosion' has meant the fragmentation of knowledge, the triumph of specialization under the guise of professionalism ... It has turned the academics away from the university, made them over into men of affairs and entrepreneurs for whom the university is merely a base, a part-time employer, and a focus of partial allegiance."[13]

Livingstone (1974) expresses that "it is part of our overall argument that a prevailing characteristic of universities today is their diversity. Part of this diversity is a growth of specialization. The teacher of today will be more specialised than ten years ago and certainly more than in twenty years ago. His department will be larger and more self contained. His relations with other departments and with the central administration will be more formalised than previously. A consequence of this process of specialization and formalization is often the growth of what can be called professionalization ... he identifies with the discipline and not with the university."[14]

Ross states that "in the balance of teaching and research, the concept of 'teacher-scholar' has meant a dual obligation which Professors were assumed to balance in a manner that permitted neither responsibility to suffer. But it was increasingly apparent that for many Professors teaching was a lesser attraction and a neglected responsibility. One careful and revealing study of the priorities of American Professors indicated a very high rating for academic freedom and pure research."[15]

The UNESCO accounts the following factors contributing to the changing role of the faculty —

1. Changes in the social context of higher education,

2. Changes in the content of the discipline, the emergence of new disciplines and inter-disciplinarity,

3. Changes in the characteristic of students,

4. Changes in the technology, particular changes in communication and information technology, and

5. Changes in theories of teaching and learning.[16]

Kerawalla (1991) has elaborately dealt with the societal changes and demands on teacher role of the present day on the following grounds.[17]

1. Role in student development,
2. Role in institutional effectiveness,
3. Role in attaining the goals of the educational system,
4. Role in national development, and
5. Role in development of the discipline.

Information Generation Among University Teachers

University academicians are not only the teachers but also scientists. Before the two World Wars, the activity of the teacher was confined to conducting classes and teaching. But the Post-War period began to see a researcher and scientist in the university teacher. The effect of the Wars on the government alerted to accelerate the development in various fields viz., science and technology, agriculture, industry, defence, etc., to build up the power of the country in the world. In most of the countries, universities being under the direct control of the government, the impact of the Wars was also seen on their objectives and goals. The activities of the

universities began to change from mere teaching to teaching and research. From this era the university faculty was not only considered as a teacher but also as scientist. The teacher realised and began to see the social problems and needs of the nation and spread his research activities to solve them. This led to the generation of new information, useful for the welfare of the society.

In American universities, the publication of articles, research outputs were taken into account while considering a teacher for promotion to higher position. The teacher without any creativity to his credit was forced either to be in the same position or to leave the job. So the teachers used to get appointments on contract basis with certain conditions.

"Publication indeed had become a guiding interest of new academician. Each book, each article was a notch pegged on the way to promotion ... This form of academic accounting not only had its public relations purposes but it served as a prod to the slow performers. It made clear who was to be promoted, when and why. 'Publish or Perish', the slogan became, and by the late 19th Century at the University of Pennsylvania Professors who insisted on pouring time and energy into teaching at the expense of research were told to go elsewhere."[18]

Such were the conditions of the Nineteenth Century in American colleges and universities. Research activities were considered as the primary duty of the teaching community, while teaching occupied the second position.

Gross and Grambsch (1974) express that "one of the most publicized issues in American education system has been that of taching versus research. The doctrine of 'Publish or Perish' typifies the controversy. The term productivity has been generally interpreted as research output and not as a balance of teaching, research and service." They further add that "it is difficult to measure productivity, even using our narrower definition, when taken as a whole."[19] The measures they have chosen are —

1. Volume of contract research;
2. Percentage of graduate student body; and
3. Number of doctorates awarded.

Lehrer (1970) comments that "when hard pressed, the educator in many instances, will have his teaching load substantially reduced to cope with the publishing race. Administrations will often gladly agree to this–indeed urge him to do so for his crowned efforts will be reflected in the University's dearly cherished 'University Image'. The educator then will rely more upon assistants to do his teaching, so that he may do research leading to publication... On the one hand, one realizes that 'he who rests, rusts', that competition is the father of all achievement, that scholar, in addition to sharing his knowledge should enrich it by investigation and the results ought to be made known to the largest possible number of interested scholars. On the other hand, one cannot deny that a full teaching schedule, with its many demands on the faculty, rarely allows a man to indulge in thorough research to be displayed in learned treatise and books. True there are research scholars who are both excellent teachers and authors."[20]

"This impulse towards quantity of publications tends to be particularly evident in the United States, owing to the system of tenure adopted in the universities there. The 'up-or-out' rule insists that university staff in the lower ranks should only be allowed a fixed number of years to show their ability, if not promoted by the end of this period, they are required to leave."[21] Thus, the conditions force the academic community to work more and more with their subjects and publish relatively to fulfil the conditions. The allocation of grants among various departments which is based on the performance also makes them publish more, for more funds, It is natural that the urge to produce more and as quickly as possible can lead to plagiarism.

Trends in Research Activities

Nirmal Kumar Bose (1967) criticises the nature of the researchers of the present day. In general, a good scientist always keeps his mind ready for the unexpected. "But in much of the research work which is carried out in our universities today, this spirit of adventure and the desire to tread the paths which are untrodden seems to be lacking. A student who bids for his Doctoral degree, or a lecturer who tries to publish largest number of papers in order to gain a lift during the next higher vacancy, cannot afford to tread the untrodden field. He bids for safety and quantity."[22]

To tap the research findings in the universities, the Government has to make its own arrangements. Here, the UGC can be made use of as a mediator. All the research activities taken up without proper understanding of subject development and the lack of intelligence in subject selection, go mere waste. Venkataraman says that a look at some of the topics on which research has been done in the various universities reveals the following facts.

Venkataraman, being a Humanities faculty, confines his study to Humanities. "The history of a reputed company is a thesis in the faculty of Business Administration in a University. Any employee of the company can tell its history just like that ... Electronic industries in a particular district, a survey on which is the subject for a M. Phil. thesis in Economics. If the same topic is extended to a State, it forms the dissertation for Ph. D. One can find more than enough material on subjects like these in the annual publications on Indian Industries by some reputed newspapers... Apart from the proliferation of research on such flimsy subjects there is detectable and shameful plagiarism in research writings."[23]

"University faculties publish much more than college faculties and a substantial difference in faculty productivity between universities and colleges persists when other conditions are controlled."[24] This may be becasue of the better opportunities, well-equipped labs, a good collection of library and mostly the encouragement given by the professional colleagues and friends. Finally, the ambition among the faculty to cherish the image of the university where they work is also the cause that leads to more and more generation of information.

The involvement of the scientist with his subjects in directly proportional to his productivity. The high involvement of the scientist in his research activities, tends to publish more and more. Scientists in research establishment spend most of their time working at research naturally, tend to have a higher research productivity than university academics, who besides administration have teaching duties. It is also felt that the change in duties and surrounding atmosphere has an impact on creativity.[25]

Forms of Information Generation

Contributions to the academic world are often made by way of publications and a list of publications is seen by many as a tangible indication of effort in this regard. Some academics enjoy the process of publication but many find it extremely difficult. Some felt that making sense of what they had written, was part of pleasure and others felt the experience far less pleasant.[26]

Ruth and Hartley (1984) express that writing is a skill. Skills are made up of sub-routines, all of which are learned, appropriately connected and integrated through practice. Writing, like most skills, involves carrying out many different sub-routines or trying to achieve many different goals all at the same time.[27]

While agreeing that writing is a skill and aimed at achieving different goals, it can be said that in every writing there is deep involvement of the writer. Sometimes, personal experiences of the author also lead to writing. Thus, generated information by the University teachers may be seen in the following forms :

1. **Papers for Publication.** It is the common form of information generation. Teachers' activities are not confined to teaching alone. To build up their identity as said earlier among professional colleagues, teachers concentrate on creativity also. Writing of an article and getting it published is not an easy thing. Because new contributions for publication are customarily examined for acceptability by some type of refereeing system. A referee is like a judge who imposes uniform scientific standards. So the papers are subjected for thorough revisions, if needed. Sometimes, it takes six months for the publication of the paper. This referee system is seen in the USA and other foreign countries, to maintain the standards and reputation of the journals.

Hence, to publish an article, the teacher should always be in touch with the current developments in his subject to avoid repetitions and outdated generation of information.

2. **Conference Papers.** Conferences and seminars are the informal ways where scientists report their works to the group of their peers before submitting for publication. American physical scientists Garvey, et. al., (1970) through their survey have found out that the 80 percent of their sample have initially reported their research work first through the seminars and conferences. Generally, this practice leads to obtain a considerable feed-back and criticism before the paper goes to the hands of a referee.[28]

While submitting the paper to a seminar or a conference teachers are not free of their choice in the subject and most of the faculty members prefer to attend these meetings for the following reasons —

1. To bring forth new ideas in their subjects that lead to the growth of the universe of knowledge;
2. To share the views of other professional friends and colleagues;
3. To gather new information generated by others; and
4. To improve their relations with the professional members of other universities.

3. **Research Projects.** Individual Research Projects and Team Research Projects are taken up by the faculty members. The financial assistance is provided by the University Grants Commission, the Central and State Governments and other funding agencies. Through these projects, academicians produce the information in the form of research reports. In the Indian University system of education, primary importance is given to the class-room teaching. But the image of the university is evaluated on research work in general carried out on personal interest. Observations and experiments during the course of research work throw up new information and data. The process of generation of new information is cyclic, the existing information being the nutrient for the further generation of information.

4. **Research Guidance.** In addition to their personal involvement in research of their choice, university teachers are involved in supervising and guiding the researchers involved in obtaining M. Phil and Ph.D. degrees. It is a collaborative effort of the teacher and scholar. As the dissertations are sent to the experts in the subject for adjudication, teachers usually take great care in guiding the researcher starting from the selection of the topic to the findings of the results. For selection and promotions of teachers of higher cadres in Indian universities, the number of M. Phils. and Ph.Ds. awarded under the guidance of a teacher in addition to other types of information generated is taken into consideration. Such teachers will take strain on personal interest in research guidance in spite of being deeply involved in class-room teaching activity. Teachers assume each award of M.Phil. Ph.D. as a feather in their cap of scholarship. It is felt that research guidance is one of the important contributions of the university teachers for the development of the subject specialisation.

5. **Class-room Lectures.** For their regular class-work, teachers go through the books and journals that are already in the library and those coming newly into the market. Reading of articles enables them to update their knowledge and to note the developments of their subject. This enables them to inform the students about the trends of their subject growth. The value of information decreases, if the gap between knowing it and utilising it increases. To bring the gap close, teachers take more strain. They also try to fill up the gap between the text-book knowledge and the current knowledge, i.e., nascent information by regular reading of books and journals. Communication of the known things is also information generation. Thus, the teacher has become the carrier of information as well as generator.

6. **Publication of Text Books and Monographs.** Writing text-books is the other form of information generated by academic community. Revision of a text book also leads to the generation of new information. In the former Soviet Union, writing of text-books for schools and colleges was valued as involvement in research.[29]

7. **Preparation of Curriculum.** Revision or preparation of curriculum is not an easy affair. The revised curriculum brings

revolution in teaching of various subjects. This leads to the advancement in subjects leading to specialisation. In the United States, some top scientists including Nobel Laureates have also made large contributions in this regard.

Thus, publication of books, journal articles, submission of papers to seminars and conferences, guiding research works, class notes, etc., are the various forms of information generated by the University teachers. For the present study, information generated by S.V. University teachers in the following forms is taken into account. They include :

1. Ph.Ds. awarded and submitted,
2. M.Phils. awarded and submitted,
3. Books published and in the press,
4. Articles (Foreign) published and accepted,
5. Articles (Indian) published and accepted,
6. Papers published in disciplines other than their own,
7. Papers presented at conferences/seminars (Foreign), and
8. Papers presented at conferences/seminars (Indian).

The data pertaining to this aspect is presented in the analysis part of the study.

REFERENCES

1. Hommadi, Ahmed Hussain, University Administration in Developing Countries, Delhi : Indian Bibliographies Bureau, 1984. p. 39.
2. Searle, J., The Campus War, Harmondsworth, Middx : Penguin, 1972. p. 170.
3. Hommadi, Ahmed Hussain, *op.cit.*, p.39.
4. Kaysen, Carl., The Higher Learing : The Universities and the Public. Princeton, New Jersey : Princeton University Press, 1969. pp. 5-8.
5. Kerr, Clark, The Uses of the University, Cambridge, Mass.: Harvard University Press, 1963. p. 114.
6. Ranganathan, S.R., University Libraries : Then and Now, *Library Herald,* 6, 1963, p. 62.
7. India, Education Commission (1964-66) (Chairman : D.S. Kothari)

Educational Planning and National Policy, pp. 541-542.
8. Viswanathan, C.G., University Libraries of India : Principles and Policy, New Delhi : Published by the Author, 1972. p. 4.
9. Laski, H.J., The Danger of Obedience and other Essays., New York : Harper and Brothers, 1930, p. 109.
10. Jayalakshmi Indiresan, Faculty Development : Some Issues and Trends,' *University News,* 29(2), Jan. 14, 1991'., p. 29.
11. Smyth, D. McCormack., Structure for University Government to the Beginning of the 20th century. Cited in Ross, Murray G.: The University. New York; McGraw-Hill, 1976, p. 94.
12. Caston, Geoffrey,, Conflicts within University Community, *Studies in Higher Education,* 2(1), 1977. p. 4.
13. Hoffman, S., Participation in Perspective, *Decdalus*, 99(1), 1970, p. 187.
14. Livingstone, Hugh., The University : An Organisational Analysis, Glasgow : Blackie, 1974, p. 75.
15. Ross, Murray G., *op.cit*., p. 105.
16. UNESCO : Academic Staff Development in Higher Education. Report of a Regional Workshop at the University of New England, Australia, 1984.
17. Kerawalla, G.J., The Role of the Teacher : Changing Perspectives., *University News,* 29(2), 1991, pp. 25-30.
18. Rudolph, Frederick, The American College and University—A History, New York : Alfred A. Knopf, 1968, pp. 403-404.
19. Gross, Edward and Gramsch, Paul V., Changes in University Organisation 1964-71, New York : McGraw Hill Book Co., 1974, pp. 88-90.
20. Lehrer, Stanley., Leaders, Teachers and Learners in Academy : Partners in Educational Process, New York : Appleton-Century Crafts, 1970, pp. 319-320.
21. Medows, A.J., Communication in Science, London : Butterworths, 1974, p. 60.
22. Bose, Nirmal Kumar, Universities and Research. *In :* Shah, A.B. (Ed.) : Higher Education in India. Bombay : Lalvani Publishing House, 1967, p. 152.
23. Venkataraman, R., The Research Game in Universities, *The Hindu,* 2 May 1989.
24. Balu, Peter M., The Organisation of Academic Work, New York : John Wiley and Sons, 1973, p. 237.
25. Pelz, D.C. and Andrews, F.M., Scientists in Organisations, New York : John Wiley, 1966.
26. Lowenthal, D. and Wason, P.C., Academics and Their Writings, *Times Literary Supplement,* 24 June, 1977, p. 782.
27. Ruth, M. and Hartley, James, Teaching and Learning in Higher Education. London : Harper and Row, 1984, p. 251.
28. Garvey, W.D. et al. Communication in the Physical and the Social Sciences. *Science,* 170, 1970, p. 1166.
29. John, V.V., Universities and Research. *In* Shah,, A.B. (Ed) : Higher Education in India, Bombay : Lalvani, 1967, p. 157.

CHAPTER 5

INFORMATION NEEDS AND AGENCIES USED BY ACADEMIC COMMUNITY

Apart from information retrieval there is virtually no other area of information science that has occasioned as much research effort and writing as 'user studies'[1] For the development of any system or for modifications to be made in it, some feed-back is required. This is only possible with the user studies. So also in the case of library and information system, user studies have gained their importance. For the assessment of the quality and quantity of the services and their utility, user studies have become the main ingredients of the system. The psychology of the users, the behaviour in gathering information, information needs of the users, the utility of various information resources, analysis of the services based on the users'needs are among the various concepts covered in user studies.

User studies are being conducted on the behaviour of the user in seeking information, instead of the needs of the user. These studies are more useful to study the user, his psychology, the working condition, the impact of his position in the society, etc. With this the user group is studied in a better way to modify the services and tools of the information system.

According to Wilson, information seeking behaviour results from the recognition of some need, perceived by the user. That behaviour may take several forms—the user may make demands upon formal systems that are customarily defined as information systems, such as libraries, on-line services, information centres; or upon systems which may perform information functions in addition to a primary, non-information function such as estate agents' offices or car sales agencies that give current information of their field, viz. prices and models, etc. The user also seeks information from other people which is otherwise called 'information exchange'. According to him, the word 'exchange' is intended to draw attention to the element of reciprocity, recognised by Sociologists and Social Psychologists as a fundamental aspect of human interaction. In the process, failure may be experienced with system as well as when seeking information from others. Use of information according to him is evaluation to discover its relationship to the user's need.[2]

"The study of information seeking behaviour can stand on its own as an area of applied research where the motive for the investigation is pragmatically related to system design and development. A different motivation is involved if we wish to understand why the information seeker behaves as he does. This is an area of basic research and, although the resulting knowledge may have practical application, there is on necessity that it should."[3]

Defining Information Needs

The terms 'information' and 'information needs' require careful definition. The satisfaction of information needs, however, does relate such effects, in terms of the individual's receiving and processing of transmitted and previously only potential communication to his needs.

However, the concept of information need has proved to be an elusive one to define, isolate and to measure. Researchers have used the term in a variety of ways. Needs, demands, and wants have been used inter-changeably, although they may not be identical. Need is further complicated by the necessity to distinguish among expressed, unexpressed, or unfelt needs, the latter being the most difficult to identity.[4]

Krikelas (1983) has defined it as the "recognition of the existence of uncertainty." Based on information seeking behaviour, needs have been categorised as immediate needs or deferred needs.[5] Faibisoff and Ely (1976) viewed the information need as either shaped by activity, such as problem solving or decision-making; or as latent, manifest through a passive reception of information which is stored as knowledge.[6]

Information scientists have identified two types of needs, which are continually confused—substance or kinds of messages and the means or channels of delivery. Because needs are internal and vary with the individual and the situation, the object of most frequent study is user behaviour and expressed demands, the assumption being that needs are implied by demands and information seeking activities.

A difference may exist between what an individual may perceive as a need and the way it is expressed. This approach seems to indicate that formulation of a expression is influenced by some perception, which is a pre-conceived idea, about the source as much as the problem. We have, therefore, a problem of differentiating when a need is realised and how it is expressed. The latter can be studied empirically but the former is again an internalised process.[7]

Information need is thus seen as a subjective, relative concept existing only in the mind of the experiencing individual. It has been defined as the "recognition of the existence of uncertainty and described as something which prevents an individual from making progress in a difficult situation."[8]

In the process of information searching, at 'initiation', a person first becomes aware of or lack of knowledge or understanding, feelings of uncertainty and apprehension. This is the stage showing the need for information.[9]

Information Needs of the Individuals

Information needs vary from individual to individual, their working conditions, the discipline in which they are working, the time, etc.

Martyn (1974) says that different types of information needs of individuals may be identified based on the stage of project or activity.[10] Two types of information needs have been identified which are substance or kinds of messages and the means or channels of delivery. The needs are internal and vary with the individual and the situation, the object of most frequent studies is user behaviour and/or expressed demands, the assumption being that needs are implied by demands and information seeking activities.[11]

David Bawden (1986) identifies four kinds of information in particular for aiding the creative process.[12] They are—

(1) Inter-disciplinary Information;

(2) Peripheral Information;

(3) Speculative Information; and

(4) Exceptions and Inconsistencies.

The effective transfer of information across disciplinary boundaries is never an easy task, even with informal media, viz., personal contacts, etc. Problems of formal information services in inter-disciplinary areas are correspondingly greater. Pachevsky's study based on the small survey showed that 14 out of 22 American scientists working in inter-disciplinary fields rated the information services available to them as unsatisfactory, compared with only one out of 55 scientists working in an established discipline.[13] The problems accounted for were scatter of publications in the primary literature, the jargon barrier between disciplines discontinuance of subscription of inter-disciplinary journals by the libraries due to financial stringency.

Another point to emerge in the consideration of creativity is the value of peripheral, or even irrelevant material, the information around the fringe that will lead to new ideas.[14]

Individual information needs of immediate nature are the product of situational conditions and are easier to recall. A decline in information need can be attributed to either a change in the situation or the establishment of some information giving service which satisfies the need. Sometimes it so happens that the previous needs logically give rise to the present information needs. The nature of the problem has the impact on the information seeking behaviour of the individual.

Voigt (1961) observes that 'a scientist's use of information, whether from print or from other sources, arises from three different needs, viz. (*a*) the need to know what other scientists have recently done or are doing. It keeps up-to-date with the current progress of a scientist's field which is called 'current approach'; (*b*) The need is the one that comes to the scientist in course of his work for some specific piece of information. This need is directly connected with research work or the problems at hand. It is called 'every day approach'; (*c*) The need comes less often but is equally important. This is the need to find and check through all the relevant information existing on a given subject. This requirement can be called the 'exhaustive approach'.[15] This shows that different needs of the scientists at different levels make them adopt different approaches to gather the required information.

Rzasa and Moriarty (1970)[16] made a study on the "types and needs of academic library users" to determine whether the faculty, graduate and under-graduate students were homogeneous with respect to their primary and secondary reasons for visiting the library and also with respect to the library materials used. The findings with respect to faculty showed that the main interest of them for using the library facilities were to do research for a publishable paper and to read for self-improvement. The second need being to find and read material required for a course, i.e., for teaching. Scholary journals and periodicals are the primary materials used by the faculty as well as graduate students.

There are different approaches to satisfy the different needs. The need in each issue is to solve an issue. The nature of the problem is perceived to require different types of information so the seeking behaviour changes. This indicates that characteristic of the problem may be a more critical indicator of potential behaviour than various personal or work characteristics.

Individuals, indeed, want to reduce uncertainty, but they may just as well want information, instruction, release from a situation, companionship, re-affirmation of reality, of social support.[17] According to Ford (1983)[18], the extent to which information seekers transfer the information into their own knowledge structures may reflect at least in part of the extent to which they really needed the information.

Factors Influencing Information Needs

Many factors other than the existence of a need will play a part on information-seeking. They are : the importance of satisfying the need, the penalty incurred by acting in the absence of full information, the availability of information sources and the costs of using them. There may be a time delay between the recognition of the need and the information seeking acts. In the case of affective needs, neither the need nor its satisfaction may be consciously recognised by the actor, whereas a cognitive need of fairly low salience may be satisfied by chance days, months or even years after it has been recognised. Sometimes it so happens that the availability of information may bring about the recognition of a previously unrecognised cognitive need.[19]

The social situations, i.e., the situations in which information is sought and used influence the attitude of information seeking. Lin and Garvey (1972)[20] identified the type of work (e.g : researcher or teacher) as the most important factor influencing the information need. Whether the work is basic or applied and the discipline in which the person is working also are the important factors.

Crawford (1978)[21] and Paisley (1968)[22] add other factors called environmental factors such as social, political, economic and legal systems within which a person operates and inter-personal relationships as important as other factors.

Krikelas (1983)[23] observed that for many issues a great deal of information required would already exist in the individual's memory; only a small part of a person's on-going needs would produce an outward behaviour that might identify as information-seeking. The level of urgency and perceived importance of the problem would influence the pattern of information-seeking.

"The full range of human, personal needs is at the root of motivation towards information-seeking behaviour, it must also be recognised that these needs arise out of the roles an individual fills in social life. So far as specialized information systems are concerned, the most relevant of these roles is 'work role', that is the set of activities, responsibilities, etc., of an individual, usually in an organizational setting, in pursuit of earnings and other satisfaction."[24]

Further, Wilson adds, that the principal generators of cognitive needs are the performance of particular tasks and the processes of planning and decision-making. The nature of the organization, coupled with the individual's personality structure, will create affective needs such as the needs for achievement, for self-expression and self-actualization. Organizational level at which a role is performed and the 'climate' of the organization are the other factors.

Paisley (1968)[25] accounts the following factors which are likely to condition information behaviour—

(i) Available information sources;

(ii) Uses to which the information will be put;

(iii) Background, motivation, professional orientation and other individual characteristics of the users;

(iv) Social, political, economic and other systems that powerfully affect the user and his work; and

(v) Consequences of information use, e.g., productivity.

Slater and Fisher (1969)[26] attempted to ascertain the motivation for obtaining information. The results of the study showed 22 percent of individuals' need was background information. 17 percent motivated to keep up-to-date of their knowledge. Others' need for information about a process, method or technique was to carry on with a current project; to instruct, train or inform others; data equations, facts and figures for immediate use in calculations and new ideas and stimulation.

Summer, Edward G. et al., (1983)[27] observed that personal, professional and psychological attributes play varying roles in predicting source use. Attitude appears to play a major role as do position and information dissemination habits. They found that educators tend not to differ in their view of desirable characteristics of information, but position and attitude will affect their opinions to varying degrees.

Among university teachers the factors associated with information needs include—information required for day-to-day class-room work, for research work, to participate in seminars/conferences, for general awareness of the developments taking place in the concerned subject and for generating new information.

For the present study the following reasons are taken into consideration as the factors influencing the information needs among the university teaching community. They are—

(*a*) To prepare for class-room,

(*b*) General awareness of new knowledge,

(*c*) For participation in Seminars/Conferences, etc.,

(*d*) To meet the needs of promotional opportunities,

(*e*) To generate new information out of curiosity and inquisitiveness,

(*f*) To write text-books, etc.

The data pertaining to this aspect is shown in the analysis part of this study.

Agencies of Information Used by Academic Community

The intensity of the need for information decides the acquiring method and agencies of information sources used. Information generation is a cyclic process, wherein we see three ingredients viz., information sources, creator/information generator and new information that is being generated. An information source is the fundamental unit in the life cycle of information production. It is fundamental because it cannot be broken down without destroying the information.

"If it is to be reused, even by its creator, the source must be verified, mechanisms of intellectual and physical access must be added, including storage facilities and various legal, organizational and economic conditions, if present, must be addressed. Meeting these requirements constitutes the institutionalization phase of the life cycle of an information source. The interdependent set of technical, organizational, socio-economic-legal activities, taken together as one phase of the life cycle, provides continuous access to information sources and results in the establishment of an information resource"[28]

Using of information resources depends on the attitude of the seeker and the information needs of the user. Working conditions, the subject of the study and the nature of the information sought (nascent, retrospective, etc.) have the impact on the use of information resources. For example, the information needs of a scholar of Humanities vary with that of a scientist. For him the information source having retrospective coverages is more important. Works published decades ago are still definitive works for him who cannot rely on recent material alone. Whereas a scientist mostly depends on day-to-day developments, nascent information in the form of abstracts, reviews, articles, formulas, etc., required for immediate use. Thus, the types of information sources and the agencies of information sources play a key role in the cycle of information generation. The use of information products and services inherently leads to the creation of new information and the start of a new cycle as shown in Figure 5.1.

The information sources thus used to satisfy the needs of various persons are grouped into (1) formal information sources, and (2) informal information sources.

Sources of Information

To know the trend of developments in the field and the results of previous experiments, etc., the investigators make use of various information sources. These sources are grouped into formal information sources (documentary sources) and informal information sources (non-documentary sources).

Fig. 5.1

Life Cycle of Information Production

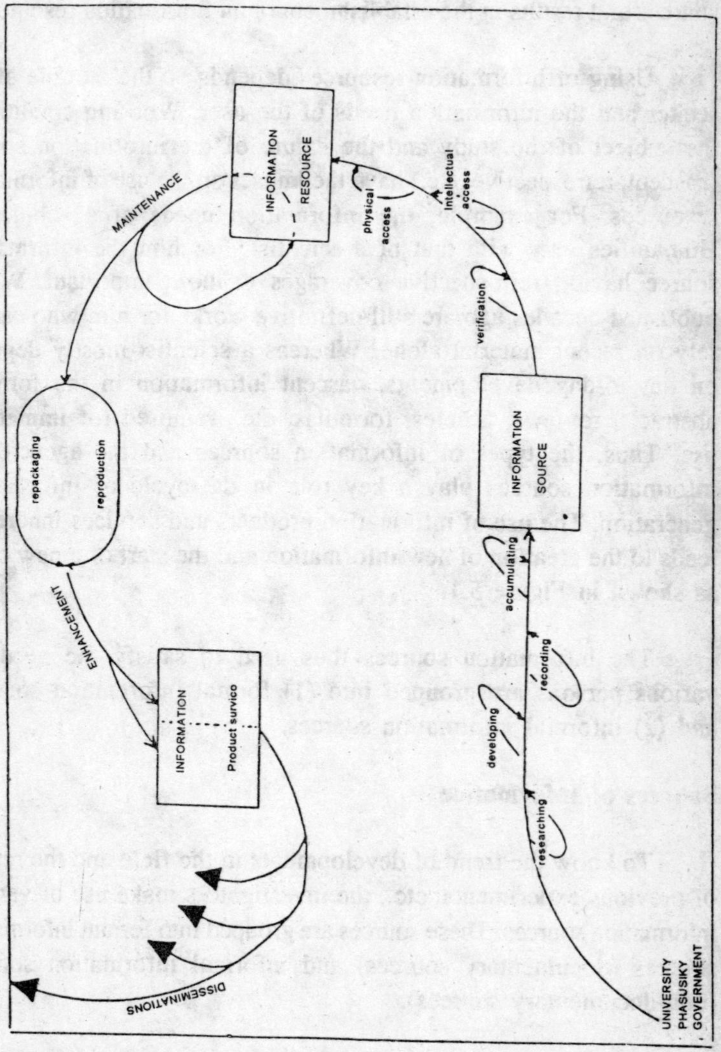

Source: Levitan Karen B. (1982)

The formal information sources are further divided into two groups based on the physical nature of document and information characteristics of the document. Formal sources include books, journals, reports, patents, abstracting and indexing journals, subject bibliographies, proceedings of conferences, surveys, etc.

The informal information sources include government departments, research organizations, learned professional societies, industries, universities, colleagues, corridor meetings at conferences, social gatherings, etc.

As already explained the use of information sources is influenced by the working conditions, subject of the study, nature of information sought, the attitude of the user and the intensity of the need one feels, etc.

Acquiring Information Through Formal Sources

There is a close relation between the activity in acquiring information and the type of need, i.e., immediate need or deferrred need. However, time plays a key-role here. It is said that activities associated with satisfying immediate needs are information-seeking behavior. Those associated with deferred needs will be defined as information-gathering behaviour. At the outset it is difficult to study the user this way in acquiring information because information need is a subjective one, relative concept existing only in the mind of the experiencing individuals. The level of urgency and perceived importance of the problem generally influence the pattern of acquiring information.

In acquiring information, the individual adopts a hierarchy of preferences, which represent some basic concept of minimal effort. Individuals prefer to get their information from a knowledgeable and perceptive source, which is known to the seeker. The next level would be to seek some one who works in an institution that clearly labels the person as being knowledgeable and probably situation-perceptive. Going through impersonal sources, i.e., literature is a common practice. Among scientists, when individuals turn to external source, they strongly prefer human contact, i.e., verbal communication.

Use of information is normally considered under two main headings—formal channels (written sources) and informal channels (usually oral). One of the major problems in making general statements about information usage by scientists lies in the difficulty of inter-comparing the results of different users, surveys. Four main approaches have been used in these studies — (*i*) questionnaire surveys, (*ii*) special diaries recording time spent in communication, (*iii*) personal interviews, and (*iv*) special observers participating with researchers. The basic intention in each case is to estimate as quantitatively as possible the relative importance of the various communication channels for the group under examination.[29]

The American Institute of Physics published in 1970 a programme for a National Information System for Physics and Astronomy 1971-75. This study made an attempt to quantify the relative importance of different information channels to Physicists Archival literarure, personal contacts, papers at meetings, non-archival literature, abstract journals and others. In the some document, comparison was made between methods of acquiring information among Physicists and Chemists. The method of following up citations in relevant papers ranked first and keeping up by reading current publications ranked second.[30]

Bernal (1948) made a study on various groups of scientists and engineers and found 5 to 15 journals being consulted by them per week. Similarly, the average number of papers read in detail varied from a low of 1.5 per week for a group of engineers to a high of 7.4 per week for scientists who were working for the Madical Research Council.[31] The factor behind the reading of various journals may be due to the spread of information and the need of the individual to keep up with a particular subject.

Further Bernal's survey showed that the British scientists used to scan the papers relating to adjacent fields of their speciality and this amounted to the quarter of their researching material and another quarter dealt with general science.

Acquiring information studied from the side of the place where the material read showed variety of behaviour of the individual. It depends on the type of employer involved, i.e., university, industry, etc., and also on the type of scientist, i.e., physicist, chemist or social scientist. Among physicists 75 percent of the reading was done in their rooms at work, 15-20 percent at home and the remaining in the library. The chemists spent 50 percent of their reading time in their rooms and 30-35 percent at home.[32]

Meadows observes two main motives behind the reasons a scientist engages in reading : (*i*) to acquire or recover specific information, the need for which has already been recognised; and (*ii*) browsing, to discover new items of information hitherto unknown.[33]

The quality of the channel has no bearing on the frequency with which the source is used and that both frequency and priority of use are determined by accessibility. Rosenberg (1967)[34] interviewed ninety-six research and non-research personnel and asked them to rank eight information gathering methods on a 7-point scale according to ease of use and amount of information expectecd and to indicate which method they would use to solve three hypothetical problems. The methods arranged in order of preference were —

1. Search personal library,
2. Search material in building where you work,
3. Visit a knowledgeable person nearby,
4. Telephone a knowledgeable person,
5. Use a library that is not within your organization,
6. Consult a reference librarian,
7. Write letter, and
8. Visit a knowledgeable person twenty miles away or more.

The study revealed the primary use of formal channels for information by ranking them first and second.

Acquiring Information Through Informal Sources

As far as informal sources of information are concerned, private correspondence is still in wide use. Oral transmission of a particular piece of information usually takes a good deal longer than written communication. But "the beginner researcher listens to literature tips by subject specialists, but carries out his research independently digging out all sorts of library and documentary material with no objection to time-consuming and redundant work.[35]

A survey of participants at a national meeting of the American Association for the Advancement of Science found the following reasons for attending the seminar, (*i*) to participate in programme, (*ii*) to acquire up-to-date information in their own specialities, (*iii*) to learn the development in related specialities, (*iv*) to learn the development in unrelated specialities, and (*v*) to learn how science and technology can serve society.[36] In general, the information collected at the conferences is of nascent in origin.- Hence, the scientists prefer to participate in meetings, and a will to travel thousands of miles for a few days of personal contact with other scientists.

Wood (1971) says that "a major reason for scientists using the informal communication network is that information passes through the network any thing up to two years before in reaches formal publication. It would appear that the only effective way of keeping up-to-date with one's subject is to develop a wide range of personal contacts or in other words, become part of what has been termed an invisible college the concept of which was first put forward by de Solla Price.[37]

The informal system often provides the line between the scientist or engineer and the formal channel. It is found particularly true in the case of engineers, most of them prefer to refer a book or article by a colleague rather than to use formal methods as an abstracting or indexing journal.[38]

In the process of collecting required information through formal as informal sources, the user depends on many agencies that provide the information sources.

Agencies of Information Sources

The information need, its kind, the channel of communication and the agency providing the source of information are inter-related.

The agencies of information sources can be grouped into two, viz., Agencies of Formal Sources and Agencies of Informal Sources.

Agencies of Formal Sources of information include —

1. Libraries :

    (*a*) Academic Libraries,

    (*b*) Special Libraries, and

    (*c*) Public Libraries.

2. Personal collections to books :

    (*a*) Self,

    (*b*) Relating to friend/colleague.

3. Information Centres :

    (*a*) National information centres,

    (*b*) International information centres.

Agencies of Informal Sources of information include —

1. Communication among small groups, they are :

    (*a*) Suggestions from colleagues/friends,

    (*b*) Contacts with peers,

    (*c*) Off-prints from authors,

    (*d*) Journal clubs,

    (*e*) Technological gate keepers, and

    (*f*) Corridor meetings at conferences.

2. Communication among big groups, they are —

    (*a*) Seminars and conferences, and

    (*b*) Invisible colleges (information exchange groups).

In the present study the following agencies of information used by S.V. University teachers have been accounted. The agencies are —

(a) Personal library,

(b) Personal collection of friends/colleagues,

(c) University library,

(d) Departmental library,

(e) Local public library,

(f) State Regional library,

(g) District Central library,

(h) Connemera Public Library (Madras),

(i) British Council Library (Madras),

(j) USIS Information Centre (Madras),

(k) Off-Prints obtained from authors, and

(l) Other agencies.

The analysed data pertaining to the above information is shown in the analysis part of this study.

REFERENCES

1. Wilson, T.D., On User Studies and Information Needs, *Journal of Documentation,* 37(1), Macrh 1981, p. 3.
2. *Ibid.*, pp. 4-5.
3. *Ibid.*, p. 7.
4. Rohde, N.F., Information Needs. *In :* Simonton, Wesley (Ed.), Advances in Librarianship, Orlando : Academic Press, 1986, Vol. 14, p. 52.
5. Krikelas, J., Information-seeking Behaviour : Patterns and Concepts, *Drexel Library Quarterly,* 19, 1983, pp. 5-20.
6. Faibisoff, S.G. and Ely, D.P., Information and Information Needs *Information Reports and Bibliographies,* 5, 1976, pp. 2-16.

7. Taylor, Robert S., Question-negotiation and Information Seeking in Libraries, *College and Research Libraries*, 29, 1968, pp. 178-194.
8. Ford, N., Knowledge Structures in Human and Machine Information Processing—Their Representation And Interaction, *Social Science Information Studies*, Vol. 3, 1983, pp. 209-222.
9. Kuhlthau, Carol C., Inside the Search Process : Information Seeking From The User's Prespective, *Journal of the American Society for Information Science*, 42(5), 1991, p. 366.
10. Martyn, J., Information Needs and Uses, *Annual Review of Information Science and Technology*, 9, 1974, pp. 3-23.
11. Menzel, H., Information Needs and Uses in Science and Technology, *Annual Review of Information Science and Technology*, 1, 1966, pp. 41-69.
12. Bawden, David., Information Systems and the Stimulation of Creativity. *Journal of Information Science*, 12, 1986, pp. 208-211.
13. Pachevsky, T., Problems of Information Services with Respect to Integration of Science, *Journal of American Society for Information Science*,. 33, 1982, pp. 115-123.
14. Martin, P., The Innovative Process and the On-line Information Channel. *In* : Stern, B.T. (Ed.) : Information and Innovation, Amsterdam : North-Holland, 1982.
15. Voigt, Melvin J., Scientist's Approach to Information, ACRL Monograph No. 24 (Chicago : American Library Association), 1961, p. 21.
16. Rzasa, Philip V. and Moriarty, John H., The Types and Needs of Academic Library Users : A Case Study of 6,568 Responses, *College and Research Libraries*, Nov. 1970, p. 407.
17. Dervin, B., Strategies for Dealing with Human Information Needs : Information or Communication, *Journal of Broadcasting*, 20, 1976, pp. 324-333.
18. Ford, N., *op.cit.*
19. Wilson, T.D., *op.cit.*, p. 8.
20. Lin, N. and Garvey, W.D., Information Needs and Uses, *Annual Review of Information Science and Technology*, 7, 1972, pp. 5-37.
21. Crawford, S., Information Needs and Uses, *Annual Review of Information Science and Technology*, 13, 1978, pp. 61-81.
22. Paisley, W.J., Information Needs and Uses, *Annual Review of Information Science and Technology*, 3, 1968, pp. 1-30.
23. Krikelas, J., *op.cit.*, pp. 5-20.
24. Wilson, T.D., *op.cit.*, p. 9.
25. Paisley, W.J., *op.cit.*, p. 9-14.

26. Slater, M. and Fisher, P., Use Made of Technical Libraries, ASLIB Occasional Publication No. 2, Aslib, 1969.
27. Summers, Edward, G., et al., The Effect of Personal, Professional, and Psychological Attributes and Information Seeking Behaviour on the Use of Information Sources by Educators, *Journal of the American Society for Information Science,* 34(1), 1983, p. 85.
28. Levitan, Karen B., Information Resources as "Goods" in the Life Cycle of Information Production, *Journal of American Society for Information Science,* January, 1982, p. 47.
29. Meadows, A.J., Communication in Science, London : Butterworths, 1974, pp. 93-94.
30. American Institute of Physics : A Program for a National Information System for Physics and Astronomy, 1971-75, Information Division, American Institute of Physics, 1970.
31. Bernal J.D., Report on the Royal Society Scientific Information Conference, Royal Society, 1948.
32. Martin, M.W. and Ackoff, R.L., *Management Science,* 9, 1963, p. 322.
33. Meadows, A.J., *op.cit.,* p. 103.
34. Rosenberg, V., Factors Affecting the Preferences of Industrial Personnel for Information Gathering Methods, *Information Storage and Retrieval,* 3(3), 1967, pp. 119-127.
35. Uytterschant, L., Literature Searching Methods in Social Science Research : A Pilot Enquiry, *American Behavioural Scientist,* 9, 1966, pp. 23-26.
36. *American Association for the Advancement of Science Bulletin,* 16, 1971.
37. Wood, D.N., *op.cit.,* p. 15.
38. Wood, D.N. and Hamilton, D.R.L., The Information Requirements of Mechanical Engineers—Report On a Recent Survey, Library Association, 1967.

PART II

DATA ANALYSIS

CHAPTER 6

INFORMATION GENERATION BY S.V. UNIVERSITY TEACHERS

All the university teachers (301) working in various departments of S.V.University College of Arts and Sciences, Tirupati who are involved in teaching and research activity, constituted the population for this study. From this a sample of 159 teachers were selected and the information was collected through a well-designed questionnaire and also through personal interview method. General information relating to age, sex, experience and the relevant aspects was collected from the subjects. The information thus collected is presented in appropriate Tables in the following pages.

In the University College, for purpose of smooth administration all the departments are grouped into the following five major schools :

1. School of Biological and Earth Sciences (SBES) : In this School the Departments included are : Bio-Chemistry, Botany, Geography, Geology, Home Science and Zoology.

2. School of Humanities and Extension Studies (SHES) : This School comprises the Departments such as : Adult Education, Education, English, Hindi, Indian Culture, Population Studies, Sanskrit, Tamil, Telugu Studies, Urdu and Philosophy.

3. School of Mathematical and Physical Sciences (SMPS) : This School consists of the Departments which are as follows: Chemistry, Mathematics Physics and Statistics.

4. School of Social and Behavioural Sciences (SSBS) : This School includes the following Departments, viz., Commerce, Economics, Econometrices, History, Law, Library and Information Science, Physical Anthropology and Prehistoric Archaeology, Physical Education, Psychology, Political Science, Public Administration, Social Anthropology and Sociology.

5. School of Business Management (SBM) : Under this School only one Department, i.e., Business Management is included.

Break up of the Respondents school-wise, cadre-wise and sex-wise is presented in Table 6.1.

Table 6.1
School-wise, Cadre-wise and Sex-wise Classification of the Respondents.

School	*Cadre of the Respondents*						*Total*	
	Professors		*Readers*		*Lecturers*			
	M	*F*	*M*	*F*	*M*	*F*	*M*	*F*
SBES	6	0	7	3	8	6	21	9
SHES	7	0	17	2	16	1	40	3
SMPS	5	0	13	1	11	0	29	1
SSBS	9	0	12	1	21	6	42	7
SBM	2	0	2	0	3	0	7	0
Total	29	0	51	7	59	13	139	20

M:Male, F:Female
Source: Survey Data.

From Table 6.1 it is clear that out of 159 respondents 18.8 percent are from SBES, 27 percent from SHES, 18.8 percent from SMPS, 30.8 percent from SSBS and 4.4 percent from SBM.

Further, it is found that among the respondents 18.2 percent are Professors, 36.4 percent Readers and 45.2 percent Lecturers.

As a whole 87.4 percent constitute male teachers and 12.5 percent female teachers. Among Readers 86.4 percent are males and 11.8 percent females. In respect of Lecturers 81.9 percent are males and 18.05 percent females.

Classification of the respondents based on their service and school to which they belong is shown in Table 6.2.

Table 6.2
Service Period of the Respondents (in Years)

School	*Service of the Respondents*				*Total*
	0-10	*11-20*	*21-30*	*Above 30*	
SBES	13	6	10	1	30
SHES	14	19	7	3	43
SMPS	10	8	9	3	30
SSBS	23	20	5	1	49
SBM	3	2	2	0	7
Total	63	55	33	8	159

Source: Computed from the Survey Data.

As far as the service period of the respondents is concerned out of 159, 39.6 percent are under 0-10 years, 34.5 percent under11-20 years, 20.75 percent under 21-30 years and the remaining 5.03 percent have over and above 30 years of service.

Age- wise and Cadre-wise distribution of the Respondents can be studied from Table 6.3.

Among Professors, 19 (65.5 percent) belong to'above 50 years' age group and 10 (34. 4 percent) 41-50 years. As for the Readers 26 (44.8 percent) are seen in 31-40 years age group, 23 (39.6 percent) in between 41-50 years and 9 (15.5 percent) 'above 50 years age group'. Among Lecturers 7 (9.7 percent) are found in 'below 30 years' age group, 53 (73.6 percent) in between 31-40' years and 12 (16.6 percent) in between 41-50' years. Irrespective of the cadre among the respondents it is seen that the highest percentage,

Table 6.3
Age-wise and Cadre-wise Classification of the Respondents

Cadre	*No. of Respondents by Age*				*Total*
Professors	0	0	10	19	29
Readers	0	26	23	9	58
Lecturers	7	53	12	0	72
Total	7	79	45	28	159

Source: Survey Data.

that is 49.6 percent is found in '31-40 years age group' and the lowest that is 4.4 percent in 'below 30 years' of age group.

Hypotheses

The following eleven hypotheses were set up to study the information generation and the library use and reading habits and such other related matters among the university teaching community :

1. Information generation, by way of writing articles, presenting papers at seminars and conferences, preparing monographs and guiding scholars leading to the award of M.Phil and Ph.D. degree is uniform among all cadres of the University teachers.
2. Information generation is not directly proportional to the experience of the teacher.
3. Sex factor has the major role to play in information generation by teaching community, i.e., both men and women faculty members are not equally good at information generation.
4. Faculty environment like team spirit among the colleagues, encouragement and healthy atmosphere in the departments will not help generate new information by the teaching community.

5. Financial assistance for research and academic work is not an important factor in information generation by the University teaching community.

6. Recognition for work is not a helpful factor in the generation of new information by the University teaching community.

7. Personal and domestic factors like health, family commitments, interaction with visitors and neighbours do not come in the way of generation of new information by the University teachers.

8. Administrative and academic burdens and problems will not hamper the generation of new information by the University teaching community.

9. For generation of new information, University teachers need not depend mainly on the university library, but make use of other library centres and personal collections.

10. University teachers who generate new information usually may not be aware of usefulness of the library and its services.

11. University teachers who generate new information do not spend more time in reading/consulting documents.

Information Generation in Relation with the Cadre of the University Teachers

The Distribution of the University teachers according to the Information Generation Index [IGI] and cadre is presented in Table 6.4.

From Table 6.4, it is evident that all Lecturers are distributed between 0-200 range of IGI, of which 90.0 percent are found under 0-100 IGI group and the remaining 10 percent under 100-200 IGI group. Whereas among Readers 98 percent are distributed in 0 to 300 IGI and the remaining 2 percent in 400-500 IGI group. In the case of Professors comparatively a fair distribution is observed. Around 72 percent are seen in 0 to 300 IGI range and the remaining

Table 6.4
Cadre-wise Distribution of the University Teachers According to the Information Generation Index (IGI)

IGI	*Cadre-wise Distribution of the Teachers*		
	Lecturers	*Readers*	*Professors*
0-100	65 (90.3)	37 (63.8)	3 (10.3)
100-200	7 (9.7)	11 (19.0)	10 (34.5)
200-300	-	9 (15.5)	8 (27.6)
300-400	-	-	4 (13.8)
400-500	-	1 (1.7)	2 (6.9)
500 and above	-	-	2 (6.9)

Note: Figures in parentheses indicate percentages.
Source: Computed from the Field Data.

28 percent in 300 and 500 IGI range. 100-200 IGI range can be considered as the turning point, from where the distribution of the number of teachers is found decreasing. From the data it may be further noticed that a high percentage of teachers is seen in the lower range of IGI and a low percentage in the higher IGI groups.

On the whole, it is clear that information generation is not the same among all the cadres. The gradual increase in the performance of the teachers, with regard to creativity, is observed from Lecturer cadre to Professor cadre.

The contents of the Table are represented in Figure 6.1.

Further consistency in information generation is studied among the three cadres of the teachers and the data is illustrated in Table 6.5.

The lower the dispersion rate the higher is the consistency in performance. In these terms Professors are found to be more consistent than Readers and Lecturers. Interestingly, the inconsistency is high among Readers as compared to that of Lecturers.

Data on cadre-wise generation of information of a person was not forthcoming. When the respondents were personally approached

Fig. 6.1

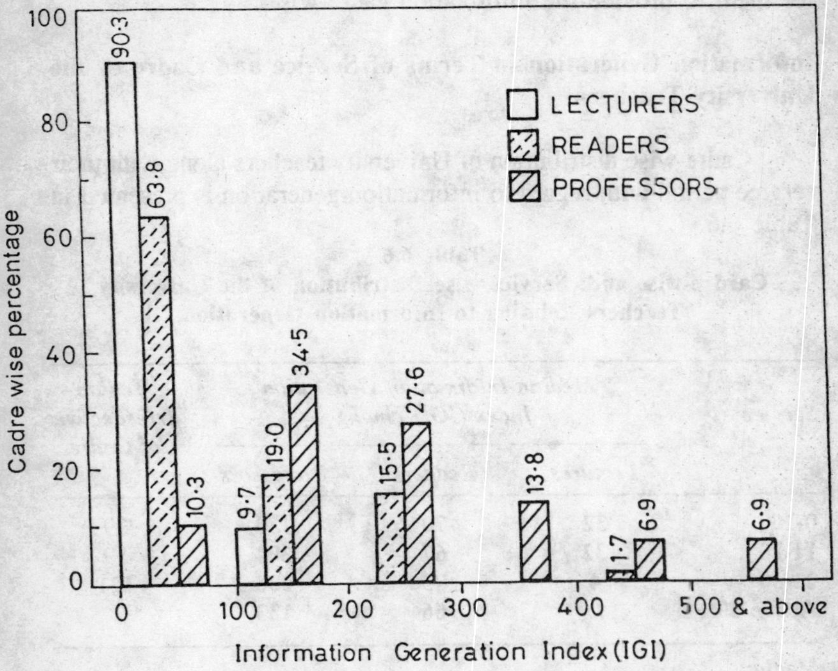

Cardre-wise Distribution of University Teachers According to Information Generation Index (IGI)

Table 6.5
Cadre-Versus Creativity: Coefficient of Dispersion

Cadre	*No. of Respondents*	*Medium Score*	*Dispersion Rate(%)*
Professors	29	20.9	41.09
Readers	58	70.5	66.16
Lecturers	72	30.5	52.50

Source: Computed from the Survey Data.

and information was sought, as they were not filling this aspect of the questionnaire many of the respondents felt that it was difficult for them to provide the information cadre-wise.

Information Generation in Terms of Service and Cadre of the University Teachers

Cadre-wise distribution of University teachers along with their service period with regard to information generation is presented in Table 6.6.

Table 6.6
Cardre-wise and Service-wise Distribution of the University Teachers Relating to Information Generation

Service	*Median Information Generation Index (IGI) among*			*Median Irrespective of Cadre*
	Lectures	*Readers*	*Professors*	
0-10	32	70	139	39
11-20	32	67	304	59
21-30	4	93	208	121
Above 30*		66	133	92.5
Median Irrespective of *Service*	30.5	70.5	209	

* The maximum service that a university teacher possess is around 36 years wich is taken as 40 to serve as approximate upper limit for graphical purpose only. (Fig. 6.2).

Source: Computed from the Survey Data.

Table 6.6 indicates the median IGI for the University Teachers in two directions i.e., cadre-wise and service-wise. It is clear that the IGI increases as the service increases irrespective of the cadre until 30 years of service. In case of the teachers whose service exceeds 30 years the value of the average IGI is found decreased.

Irrespective of the service, the average IGI increased with cadre. The median IGI for Professors is roughly seven times to that

Fig. 6.2

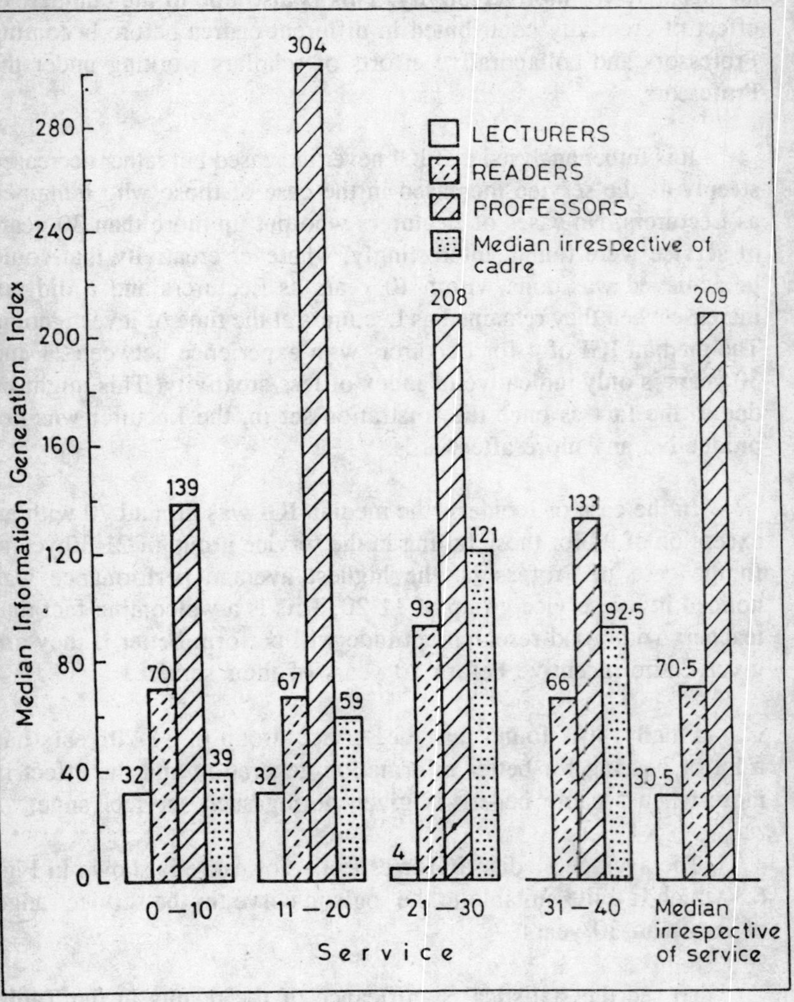

Cadre-wise and Service-wise Distribution of University Teachers Relating to Information Generation

of the Lecturers. This perhaps is due to the effect of the cadre as an incentive for more creativity. This is also due to the cumulative effect of creativity contributed in different cadres before becoming Professors and collaborative efforts of scholars working under the Professors.

It is futher analysed that IGI never increased but rather decreased steeply as the service increased in the case of those who remained as Lecturers. No cases of Lecturers who put up more than 30 years of service were found. Interestingly, whatever creativity that could be achieved was done within 10 years as Lecturers and it did not increase when they remained as Lecturers at the time of investigation. The median IGI of 4 for Lecturers with experience between 21 and 30 years is only indicative of index of less creativity. This might be due to the fact as once the frustration set in, the Lecturer was not productive any more afterwards.

In the case of Readers, the median IGI was around 70 with an exception of 93 for those falling in the service group of 21-30 years. In the case of Professors, the highest average performance was noticed in the service group of 11-20. This is a welcoming fact that teachers with good research aptitude will perform better if they are given cadre incentive before 20 years of their service.

Finally, it is found that the service group of 11-20 years has a lot of bearing for better information generation and the effect is more when a cadre benefit is given during such service range.

The average median IGI irrespective of cadre is shown in Fig. 6.3 which is quite suitable to the logistic curve, in the service range of less than 30 years.

To see the statistical significance of the results in the Table the following statistical null hypothesis is framed towards a possible rejection based on the data with the specified confidence of making a correct decision.

H_0 : With respect to the information generation service of the teachers and cadres are independent attributes.

Fig. 6.3

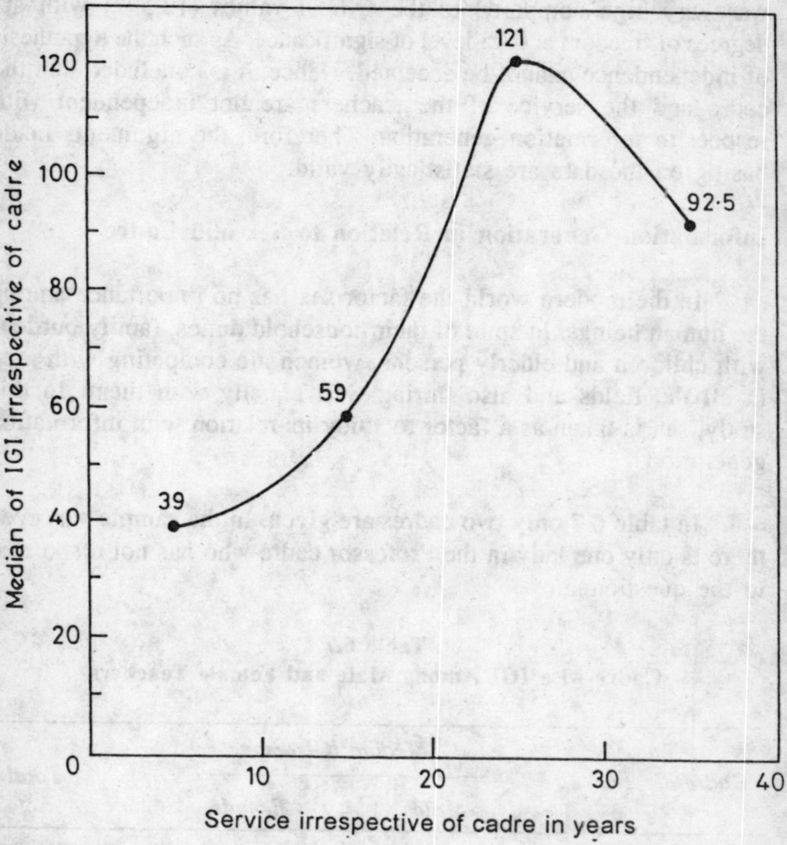

Average Information Generation Among Teachers in Terms of Service

From the data in Table 6.6 the independent variable was tested by using chi-square test. The computed value of chi-square 63.7235 was very high compared to the critical values (12.592) with six degrees of freedom at 0.05 level of significance. As such the hypothesis of independence cannot be accepted. Hence, it is concluded that the cadre and the service of the teachers are not independent with respect to information generation. Therefore, the arguments made basing on the data are statistically valid.

Information Generation in Relation to Sex and Cadre

In the modern world the factor sex has no importance among the human beings. In spite of their household duties, family burdens with children and elderly persons, women are competing with men in all the fields and also fairing well equally with them. In this study, sex is taken as a factor to study its relation with information generation.

In table 6.7 only two cadres are given. In the sample surveyed there is only one lady in the Professor cadre who has not responded to the questionnaire.

Table 6.7
Cadre-wise IGI Among Male and Female Teachers

Cadre	*Median IGI among*		*Total*
	Male	*Female*	
Readers	71	35	106
Lecturers	22	33	55
Grand Total	93	68	161

Source : Survey Data.

Table 6.7 shows the average IGI for the University teachers in two directions namely sex-wise and cadre-wise. It is observed that IGI of female Lecturers is higher than that of the male counterparts. Whereas in the case of Readers, males have shown double the IGI of females.

When the IGI is compared within the sex, it is found that in the cadre of female Readers the IGI is found to be not much different from that of the female Lecturers. In the case of males, Readers have shown three times of IGI to that of the Lecturers.

It may be concluded that female Lecturers perform better before they become Readers and the creativity cannot increase in the cadre.

To see the statistical significance of the results from Table 6.7 the following null hypothesis is framed.

H_0 : With regard to the information generation, sex and cadre of the teachers are the independent attributes.

Fig. 6.4

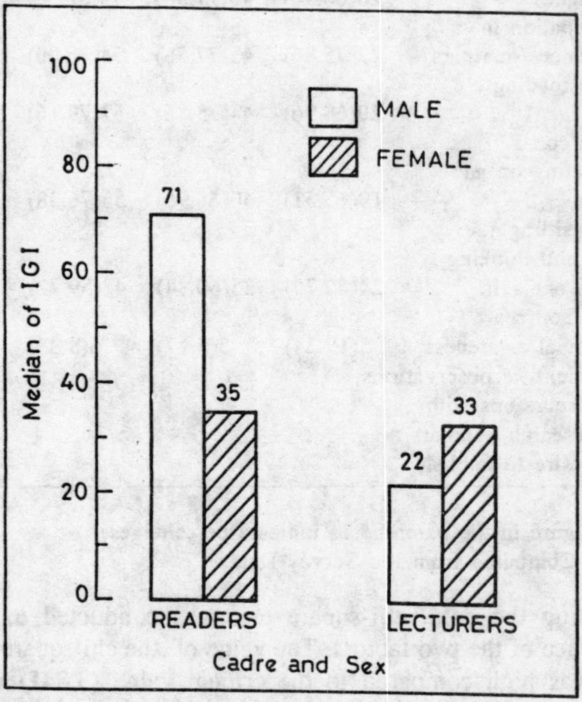

Median IGI among Male and Female Teachers

Table 6.8
Cadre-wise Classification of Teachers Inspired by Various Factors for Information Generation

Sl. No.	*Sources of Inspiration*	*Inspired Cadre-wise Respondents*			*Total*
		Professors	*Readers*	*Lecturers*	
1.	Discussion with family members	6(20.68)	7(12.06)	9(12.50)	22(13.83)
2.	Discussion with friends other than professional colleagues	9(31.03)	17(29.31)	20(27.77)	46(28.93)
3.	Discussion with professional colleagues	20(68.96)	45(77.58)	59(81.94)	124(77.98)
4.	Participation in conferences/seminars	22(75.86)	45(77.58)	54(75.00)	121(76.10)
5.	While reading a book	20(68.96)	44(75.86)	57(79.16)	121(76.10)
6.	While con-templating on an article	19(65.51)	40(68.96)	55(76.38)	114(71.69)
7.	When sitting alone and thinking within one-self	24(82.75)	35(60.34)	43(59.72)	102(64.15)
8.	Other Sources : (a) Social awareness, (b) Scientific observations, (c) Discussions with Research Scholars (d) Desire to publish.	5(17.24)	3(5.17)	6(8.33)	14(8.80)

Note : Figure in the parentheses indicate percentages.
Source : Computed from the Survey Data.

Using the data, chi-square test was conducted to test the dependence of the two factors. The value of the chi-square 10.7818 which was high compared to the critical value (3.841) with one degree of freedom at 0.05 level of significance.

This indicates that independence of sex and cadre in terms of information generation cannot be accepted. It may, therefore, be concluded that the factors, sex and cadre, are related and play a key role in information generation.

Sources of Inspiration for Information Generation

Discussion with friends and colleagues, serious reading of books, group discussions, participation in seminars and conferences are the sources for inspiring a person towards new ideas for generating new information. These and a few other sources of inspiration are studied among the University teachers and the data is presented in Table 6.8.

On rearrangement of the inspiring sources according to the percentage of totals irrespective of the cadres, the awarded ranks are shown in Table 6.9.

Table 6.9
Ranking of Inspiring Sources

Sl. No.	*Inspiring Sources*	*Rank*
1.	Discussion with professional colleagues	1
2.	Participation in conferences/seminars	2
3.	While reading a book	2
4.	While contemplating on an article	3
5.	While sitting alone and thinking within one-self	4
6.	Discussion with friends other than professional colleagues	5
7.	Discussion with family members	6
8.	Other sources	7

By dividing the teachers into two broad groups, viz., passive and active, the former is inspired by human beings (viz., colleagues, friends, family members, participation in Conferences/Seminars and the latter by documents (viz., reading of books, journals and other factors). The findings of the study clearly show an unequal distribution of teachers between these two broad groups. From the percentages of the aggregate it can be inferred that 64.6 percent of the teachers fall under passive group and 35.3 percent under active group.

CHAPTER 7

FACTORS INFLUENCING INFORMATION GENERATION AMONG S.V. UNIVERSITY TEACHERS

Factors Helping in Information Generation

The following three major factors are identified as helpful in information generation for the University teachers. They are —

(*a*) Faculty Environment (FE),

(*b*) Financial Assistance (FA), and

(*c*) Recognition of the Work (RW).

To study the significance of the impact of these factors Chi-square technique was used by framing the following null hypothesis.

H_0 : All the helpful factors for information generation among University teachers are alike.

If this hypothesis is true, one can expect an equal number of cases under each factor as shown in Table 7.1.

The calculated chi-square value 67.771, which is far greater than the critical value (5.99) with two degrees of freedom at 0.05 level of significance shows a significant difference in the impact of these factors on information generation.

Table 7.1
Number of Teachers Claiming Each Factor as Helpful Under Helpful Factors

	Factors			*Total*
	FE	*FA*	*RW*	
Observed values	112	28	41	181
Expected values	60.33	60.33	60.33	181

Source : Computed from the Survey Data.

The calculated chi-square value 67.771, which is far greater than the critical value (5.99) with two degrees of freedom at 0.05 level of significance shows a significant difference in the impact of these factors on information generation.

It is observed that the factor 'Faculty Environment' is primarily claimed as the helping factor in information generation by 112 teachers (70 percent). The factors 'Financial Assistance' is claimed by 28 teachers (16 percent) and 'Recognition of work' by 41 teachers (25.8 percent). This shows that the factor 'Faculty Environment' is more influential than the other two factors and the factor 'Recognition of the Work' is more influential than the factor 'Financial Assistance' among the teachers.

These factors were studied separately to find the impact on information generation among the three cadres of the University teachers.

Faculty Environment

Within the faculty environment three major factors were identified as helpful for information generation which were given top priority by the teachers. These are—

(*a*) Healthy Atmosphere in the Faculty (HA),

(*b*) Encouragement from Colleagues (EC), and

(c) Team Research Spirit (TRS)

Chi-square technique was employed to study the impact of these factors on information generation irrespective of the cadre of the teachers (Table 7.2).

H_0 : All the faculty environment factors are equally claimed by the teachers as helpful factors.

If this hypothesis is true, one can expect an equal number of cases under each factor, as shown in Table 7.2.

Table 7.2
Number of Teachers Claiming Faculty Environmental Factors Helpful for Information Generation

	Factors			*Total*
	HA	*EC*	*TRS*	
Observed values	74	21	17	112
Expected values	37.33	37.33	37.33	112

Source : Computed from the Survey Data.

The calculated chi-square value is 54.23, which is greater than the critical value (5.99) with two degrees of freedom at 0.05 level of significance. Hence, H_0 is rejected, indicating the significant difference in the impact of these factors on information generation.

The factor 'Healthy Atmosphere' is the faculty being claimed by 74 teachers (46.54 percent) shows its primary importance over 'Encouragement from Colleagues' claimed by 21 teachers (13.2 percent) and 'Team Research Spirit' by 17 teachers (10.69 percent) as helpful factors in information generation among University teachers.

Further, the impact of these factors was studied cadre—wise and the analysed data is represented in Table 7.3.

From Table 7.3, it is evident that 'Healthy Atmosphere' is almost equally claimed by each cadre of the teachers (about 46.8 percent) as a helpful factor in information generation. The factor

Table 7.3
Impact of Faculty Environment Factors on Information Generation among the Cadres of the University Teachers

Factor	*Cadre-wise Distribution of Teachers Among the Factors*			*Total*
	Professors	*Readers*	*Lecturers*	
HA	14(48.28)	26(44.82)	34(47.22)	74(46.8)
EC	2(6.89)	7(12.06)	12(16.66)	21(11.8)
TRS	3(10.34)	6(10.34)	8(11.11)	17(10.6)
Grand Total :	19(65.51)	39(67.24)	54(75.00)	112(69.2)

Note: Figures in the parentheses indicate percentages.
Source : Computed from the Survey Data.

'Team Research Spirit' is also equally claimed by about 10.6 percent of the teachers of each cadre. This indicates that the former may be considered as the primary factor.

In comparison, the factor 'Encouragement from Colleagues' has shown a low percentage (6.89 percent) among Professors, whereas a relatively high percentage (16.66 percent) among Lecturers. This is natural because Professors being seniors in the profession usually do not require encouragement from their juniors. Whereas, Lecturers being juniors and usually younger in age and experience require encouragement in all aspects.

An overall responses structure however reveals that irrespective of the cadres, about 47 percent of the respondents are in favour of healthy atmosphere as the primary means of information generation. The other two factors are treated as important by only 22.00 percent of the respondents. It, however, does not mean that these three factors are ignored by other respondents, but only reflects the individual's priority towards each of these factors. For such respondents these factors occupy a lower priority. It can be concluded that 69 percent of the respondents having claimed 'Faculty Environment' as the helpful factor for generating information indicates its significance with regard to the University atmosphere.

Financial Assistance

Within the financial assistance two major factors are identified as helpful factors in generating information, which are given top priority. They are—

(a) Help by way of liberal finances to undertake research (LF), and

(b) Assistance of Publication (AP).

To study the impact of these factors on information generation among the University teachers, chi-square technique was employed by framing the null hypothesis as follows :

H_0 : Both the factors relating to 'Financial Assistance' are felt equally helpful for information generation among the University teachers.

If this hypothesis is true, one can expect an equal number of cases under each factor, as shown in Table 7.4.

Table 7.4
Number of Teachers Claiming for Financial Assistance as a Helping Factor

	Factors		*Total*
	LF	*AP*	
Observed values	21	7	28
Expected values	14	14	28

Source : Computed from Survey Data.

The calculated chi-square value 7.0 is greater than the critical value (3.84) with one degree of freedom at 0.05 level of significance.

Rejection of H_0 thus shows the significant difference in the impact of these factors on information generation.

The factor 'Liberal Finance to Undertake Research' is claimed by 21 teachers (13.2 percent) and the other factor 'Assistance for Publication' by 7 teachers (4.4 percent), as helpful factors in information generation.

The impact of these factors on information generation was studied cadre-wise. The exact number and the percentage (within brackets) of teachers claiming each of these factors as helpful in information generation is presented in Table 7.5.

Table 7.5
Impact of Financial Assistance Factors on Information Generation Among the University Teachers

Factor	Cadre-wise Distribution of Teachers			
	Professors	Readers	Lecturers	Total
LF	2(6.89)	8(13.79)	11(15.27)	21(11.98)
AP	1(3.44)	2(3.44)	4(5.55)	7(4.14)
Grand Total	3(10.34)	10(17.24)	15(20.83)	28(16.12)

Source : Computed from Survey Data.

It is evident from Table 7.5 that the cadre-wise difference in percentage of cases, irrespective of factor is high among Lecturers. This shows that Lecturers are claiming 'Financial Assistance' as the helpful factor in information generation. On the whole, irrespective of the cadre, about 16 percent of the respondents are in favour of this factor. The low percentage does not mean that it is ignored by other respondents, but reflects the individual priority. For such respondents these factors occupy a lower priority.

Further, it follows the 'Liberal Finance to Undertake Research' is the highly preferred factor for information generation, irrespective of the cadre. Interestingly, the same factor is claimed as helpful by more number of Lecturers than Professors and Readers. Again Assistance of Publication' is also more claimed to the another major factor for information generation by Lecturers than Professors and Readers. Therefore, it may be concluded that for those teachers aspiring higher academic positions, the factor 'Financial Assistance' is of great use, resulting in more information generation.

Recognition of the Work

'Recognition of the Work' (RW) is also given top priority as a helpful factor for information generation. The percentage of teachers claiming this as a helping factor by giving top priority is shown cadre-wise in Table 7.6.

Table 7.6
Impact of 'Recognition of Work' on Information Generation Among University Teachers

Factor	Cadre-wise Distribution of Teachers			
	Professors	Readers	Lecturers	Total
RW	7(24.13)	11(18.96)	23(31.94)	41(25.01)

Note : Figures in parentheses indicate percentages.

Source : Computed from Survey Data.

The responses as evident from the data in Table 7.6 show that there is a fair difference in the percentage among the three cadres. Lecturers, the emerging group in the academic field, expressed the need of recognition of the work with a high percentage (31.94 percent). Surprisingly, 24.13 percent of Professors also felt of the same along with Readers (18.96 percent) in treating the factor as helpful in information generation.

Irrespective of the cadre, among the factors that were given first priority as helpful for information generation 'Recognition of Work' is found to be favoured by 25 percent.

Influence of Domestic Factors on Information Generation among the University Teachers

The attitude and livelihood of the human beings are influenced by social factors. The ability of thinking and decision-making enabled man to overcome these problems and lead a normal life. However, the influence of these factors retard the progress in his life. Working employees face the problems from multidirections within their working organisation, the family and the society. In this lstudy these factors are grouped into : (*a*) Domestic factors, and (*b*) Academic and official factors, which come in the way of information generation among the University teachers.

Domestic Factors include the following—

1. Size of the family (SF)
2. Education of the dependents (ED)
3. Marriages of the dependents (MD)
4. Attitude of the family members (AFM)
5. Health problems of family members (HPF)
6. Personal health problems (PHP)
7. Frequent journies leaving the headquarters (FJ)
8. Frequent visits of the relatives (FV) (Tirupati being a pilgrim centre)
9. Problems with relatives (viz., land disputes, legal disputes, etc.) (PR)
10. Problems with neighbours (PN)
11. Other Domestic Factors if any (ODF).

The frequent visits of friends and relatives will normally have impact on the family. Tirupati, being a pilgrim centre, more number of relatives and friends, frequently, visit to have the *darshan* of Lord Balaji at Tirumala Hills. This ultimately influences the host and the members of his family. As such this factor is particularly taken into consideration as influencing one on information generation by the university teachers. The analysed data is presented in Table 7.7.

Chi-square technique was used to study the impact of domestic factors on information generation among the University teachers. For this the following null hypothesis was framed.

H_0 : All the domestic factors have the same impact on information generation among the University teachers.

Table 7.7

Number of Teachers Claiming Influence of each Domestic Factor on Information Generation

	Factors											
	SF	*ED*	*MD*	*AFM*	*HPF*	*PHP*	*FJ*	*FV*	*PR*	*PN*	*ODF*	Total
Observed values	26	35	19	21	42	37	25	43	23	10	6	287
Expected values	26.09	26.09	26.09	26.09	26.09	26.09	26.09	26.09	26.09	26.09	26.09	287

Source : Computed from the Survey Data.

If this hypothesis is true, one can expect an equal number of cases under each factor, as shown in Table 7.7.

The calculated chi-square value 56.986 is greater than the cirtical value (18.31) with ten degrees of freedom at 0.05 level of significance.

This indicates variation in the impact of the domestic factors on information generation.

The data is further analysed to study the impact of these factors on information generation among various cadres of the teachers Table 7.8.

Table 7.8
Impact of Domestic Factors Viewed as Unhelpful for Information Generation Among Various Cadres of the Teachers

Sl. No.	*Domestic Factors*	*No. of Teachers Claiming Cadre-wise*			
		Professors	*Readers*	*Lecturers*	*Total*
1.	Large family to look after	6 (20.6)	7 (12.0)	13 (18.0)	26 (16.35)
2.	Education of the dependents	7 (24.13)	13 (22.4)	15 (20.8)	35 (22.01)
3.	Marriages of the dependents	4 (13.7)	8 (13.7)	7 (9.7)	19 (11.94)
4.	Attitude of the family members	3 (10.3)	8 (13.7)	10 (13.8)	21 (13.20)
5.	Health Problems of the family members	6 (20.6)	15 (25.8)	21 (29.1)	42 (26.41)
6.	Personal health problems	7 (24.13)	14 (24.1)	16 (22.2)	37 (23.27)
7.	Frequent journies leaving headquarters	4 (13.7)	8 (13.7)	13 (18.0)	25 (15.72)
8.	Frequent visits of friends/relatives	2 (6.8)	21 (36.2)	20 (27.7)	43 (27.04)

9.	Problems with relatives	3 (10.3)	8 (13.7)	12 (16.6)	23 (14.46)
10.	Problems with neighbours	0	5 (8.6)	5 (6.9)	10 (6.28)
11.	Other domestic factors	1 (3.4)	3 (5.1)	2 (2.7)	6 (3.77)

Figures in the parentheses indicate the percentages.
Source : Computed from the Survey Data.

The responses as presented in Table 7.8 point out that of all the domestic factors, 'Frequent visits of friends and relatives' is claimed by the highest number of teachers (27.04 percent). This indicates that this is a highly influencing factor on information generation among the teachers. 26.41 percent of the teachers claimed 'Health problems of the family' as influencing one on information generation, thus indicating its secondary importance. 'Personal health problems' and 'Education of the dependents' are the other two major factors which influenced 23.27 percent and 22.01 percent of the teachers, respectively.

The cadre-wise study of the percentages among the factors indicates that 'Education of the dependents' as well as 'Personal health problems' are the primary factors hampering information generation among the University Professors. In case of Readers, it is 'Frequent visits of friends and relatives', which is primarily influencing the act of information generation, whereas, among Lecturers it is 'Health problems of the family members'.

To find out the vital domestic factors, 15.72 percent in the aggregate percentages is taken as a cut-off point. Factors with percentages above 15.72 percent are grouped under 'vital factors' and the remaining are treated as 'non-vital factors', which are listed as follows —

Vital Factors include

(*a*) Frequent visits of friends and relatives;

(*b*) Health problems of the family members;

(*c*) Personal health problems;

(*d*) Education of the dependents; and

(*e*) Large family to look after.

Non-vital Factors include

(*a*) Frequent journies leaving headquarters;

(*b*) Problems with relatives (viz. land disputes, legal disputes, etc.);

(*c*) Attitude of the family members;

(*d*) Marriages of the dependents;

(*e*) Problems with neighbours, and

(*f*) Other factors viz.,

(*i*) Laziness

(*ii*) Spouse employed

(*iii*) Financial burden.

Influence of Academic and Official Factors on Information Generation Among the University Teachers

The influence of the academic and official factors was studied on information generation. One needs a pleasant atmosphere both in and out of his home for better performance. The act of information generation being a mental process, even a small disturbance in the surroundings shows its impact on the creator and creativity.

Academic and official factors that could be unhelpful for information generation are as follows :

(1) Headship (HS)

(2) Chairmanship of Board of Studies (CBS)

(3) Evaluation work (EW)

(4) Research guidance (RG)

(5) Teacher activity (Burden of work load) (TA)

(6) Problems with the higher officials (PWH)

(7) Problems with colleagues (PWC)

(8) Problems with the students (PWS)

(9) Other related problems if any (OAF).

The impact of the academic and official factors on information generation was studied by employing chi-square technique. The following null hypothesis was framed for this purpose.

H_0 : All the academic and official factors have the same impact on information generation among the University teachers.

If this hypothesis is true, one can expect an equal number of cases under each factors as shown in Table 7.9.

Table 7.9
Number of Teachers Claiming Each Academic and Official Factors Unhelpful

	Factors									*Total*
	HS	*CBS*	*EW*	*RG*	*TA*	*PWH*	*PWC*	*PWS*	*OAF*	
Observed values	28	3	18	43	52	32	33	17	17	243
Expected values	27	27	27	27	27	27	27	27	27	243

Source : Computed from the Survey Data.

The calculated chi-square value 66.663 is greater than the critical value (15.51) with eight degrees of freedom at 0.05 level of significance.

This shows the unequal impact of the academic and official factors on information generation among the University teachers.

The study is further extended to find out the impact of these factors among the cadres relating to information generation (Table 7.10).

Table 7.10

Views of Academic and Official Factors as Unhelpful for Information Generation among the Various Cadres of the Teachers

Sl. No.	*Academic and Official factors*	*No. of teachers claiming cadre-wise*			
		Professors	*Readers*	*Lecturers*	*Total*
1.	Headship	9 (31.0)	14 (24.1)	5 (6.9)	28 (17.61)
2.	Chairmanship of Board of Studies	3 (10.3)	0	0	3 (1.88)
3.	Evaluation work	3 (10.3)	6 (10.3)	9 (12.5)	10 (11.32)
4.	Research guidance	5 (17.2)	20 (34.4)	18 (25.0)	43 (27.04)
5.	Teaching Activity (Burden of workload)	7 (24.1)	19 (32.7)	26 (36.1)	52 (32.7)
6.	Problems with the higher officials	3 (10.3)	12 (20.6)	17 (23.6)	32 (20.12)
7.	Problems with colleagues	3 (10.3)	15 (25.8)	15 (20.8)	33 (20.75)
8.	Problems with the students	4 (13.7)	6 (10.3)	7 (9.7)	17 (10.69)
9.	Other factors	2 (6.8)	6 (10.3)	9 (12.5)	17 (10.69)

Figures in the parentheses indicate the percentages.
Source : Computed from the Survey Data.

On observation of the data from Table 7.10, it is inferred that Professors (31 percent) have claimed 'Headship' as the primary factor affecting their activity in generating new information. In case of Readers (34.4 percent) the impact is felt mainly due to 'research guidance', whereas among Lecturers (36.1 percent), the 'burden of work load due to teaching activity', found primarily hampering information generation.

Further, it may be noted that a low percentage (24.1 percent) of Readers and a least percentage among Lecturers (6.9 percent) have claimed 'Headship' as unhelpful factor. This is because, headship is rotated among Professors and Readers for every two years in the university departments whereas in some of the departments, the responsibility is extended up to Lecturer cadre also (e.g., Library and Information Science, Philosophy) taking the service as the base for seniority into consideration. At the same time no responses are found from Readers and Lecturers to the factor 'Chairmanship of Board of Studies' as the Chairmanship is pertained to Professor cadre only.

A total of 32.7 percent of the teachers irrespective of their cadre were found primarily affected by the 'Teaching activity' in information generation. Performance of information generation among 27 percent of the teachers was reported to be hampered due to 'Research guidance'. The factors 'Problems with professional colleagues' and 'Problems with higher officials' came in the way of information generation among 20.0 percent of the teachers.

To find out the vital factors and non-vital factors, the median 17.61 in the aggregate percentage is taken as a cut-off point. Factors with percentages above 17.61 percent are grouped under "Vital factors" and the remaining under "Non-Vital factors". These are listed as follows.

Vital Factors

(*a*) Burden of workload due to teaching activity,

(*b*) Research guidance,

(*c*) Problems with colleagues, and

(*d*) Problems with higher officials.

The vitality of the latter two factors clearly indicates the existence of unhealthy atmosphere in the departments and in the institution as a whole, hampering the performance of information generation among the University teachers.

Non-vital factors

(*a*) Headship,

(*b*) Evaluation work,

(*c*) Problems with students,

(*d*) Other factors viz.,

  (*i*) extra responsibilities and correspondences,

  (*ii*) no job satisfaction,

  (*iii*) other assignments by administration, and

(*e*) Chairmanship of Board of Studies.

CHAPTER 8

AGENCIES OF INFORMATION SOURCES USED BY THE S.V. UNIVERSITY TEACHERS

Agencies of Information Sources Used

The following agencies for information are taken as sources for study to observe their usage among the University teaching community.

(1) Personal Library (PL),

(2) Departmental Library (DL),

(3) University Library (UL),

(4) Local Public Library (LPL),

(5) State Regional Library (SRL),

(6) District Central Library (DCL),

(7) Connemera Public Library (Madras) (CPL),

(8) British Council Library (Madras) (BCL),

(9) USIS Information Centre (Madras) (USIS),

(10) Personal Collection of Friends and Colleagues (PCF),

(11) Off-prints obtained from Authors (OP), and

(12) Other agencies (OA).

The significant usage of these agencies was tested by using chi-square technique and for this the following null hypothesis was framed.

H_0 : All the information sources are equally used by the University Teachers.

If this hypothesis is true, one can expect an equal number of cases under each factor. This is presented in Table 8.1.

The calculated chi-square value 465.167 is greate than the critical value 58.25 with eleven degrees of freedom at 0.05 level of significance.

The rejection of H_o signifies the unequal use of agencies of information sources by the University teachers.

The study is further extended to find out the cadre–wise use of these agencies among the teachers, as shown in Table 8.2.

As a whole, from the data in Table 8.2, it is found that irrespective of the cadre, 96.8 percent of the respondents use the 'University Library' as an agency for collecting information, which clearly shows its primary importance. The use of 'Personal collections of documents' by 72 percent of the teachers indicates its secondary importance as an agency of information source.

Among the respondents about 64 percent make use of 'Departmental libraries' for collecting information, whereas 'Off-prints' is used by about 60 percent of the teacher respondents. 'Personal collections from friends/colleagues' are used by about 57 percent of the respondents.

As for the other sources being used by 23 percent of the respondents, they include agencies having national reputation which are as follows :

(1) S.V.U. Oriental Research Institute, Tirupati.

(2) Andhra Pradesh State Archives, Hyderabad.

Table 8.1
Use of Agencies for Information Sources among the University Teachers

	No. of Teachers Using the Agencies												Total
	PL	DL	UL	SRL	DCL	LPL	CPL	BCL	USIS	PCF	OP	OA	
Observed values	115	101	154	13	3	15	24	25	29	90	94	36	699
Expected values	58.25	58.25	58.25	58.25	58.25	58.25	58.25	58.25	58.25	58.25	58.25	58.25	6 9 9

Source: Computed from the Survey Data.

Table 8.2
Cadre-wise Use of Agencies of Information Among the University Teachers

Sl. No.	*Agencies of Information Sources*	*Cadre-wise*			*Total*
		Professors	*Readers*	*Lecturers*	
1.	Personal Library	21 (72.4)	39 (67.2)	55 (76.3)	115 (72.32)
2.	Departmental Library	15 (51.7)	35 (60.3)	51 (70.8)	101 (63.52)
3.	University Library	28 (96.5)	57 (98.2)	69 (95.8)	154 (96.85)
4.	Local Public Library	3 (10.3)	2 (3.4)	10 (13.8)	15 (9.43)
5.	State Regional Library	2 (6.8)	7 (12.0)	4 (5.5)	13 (8.17)
6.	District Central Library	1 (3.4)	0	2 (2.8)	3 (1.88)
7.	Connemera Public Library (Madras)	4 (13.7)	8 (13.8)	12 (16.6)	24 (15.1)
8.	British Council Library (Madras)	4 (13.7)	10 (16.9)	11 (15.2)	25 (15.72)
9.	USIS Information Centre (Madras)	5 (17.2)	10 (16.9)	14 (19.4)	29 (18.23)
10.	Personal collection of friends	15 (51.71)	30 (50.8)	45 (62.5)	90 (56.6)
11.	Off-prints obtained from authors	18 (62.0)	34 (57.6)	42 (58.3)	94 (59.11)
12.	Other sources	7 (24.1)	13 (22.10)	16 (22.2)	36 (22.64)

Figures in the parentheses indicate percentages.

Source : Computed from the Survey Data.

(3) Bureau of Economics and Statistics, Hyderabad.

(4) American Studies Research Centre, Hyderabad.

(5) National Institute of Nutrition, Hyderabad.

(6) National Institute of Rural Development, Hyderabad.

(7) Ramanujam Institute, Madras.

(8) Indian Institute of Technology, Madras.

(9) Adayar Library and Research Institute, Madras.

Even though the British Council Library, USIS Information Centre and Connemera Public Library are situated at Madras 15 to 18 percent of the teacher respondents visit them for their research purposes.

To find out the potential agencies based on the utility, the median 22.7 percent in the aggregate percentage is taken as the cut-off point. The potential agencies included are :

(*a*) S.V. University Library,

(*b*) Personal Libraries,

(*c*) Departmental Libraries,

(*d*) Off-prints obtained from Authors, and

(*e*) Personal collection of Friends.

Awareness of Library Services and the Frequency use of Library among the University Teachers

The utilization of resources of library and its services mainly depend on the awareness of its services among the user community. The awareness has its impact on the utilisation of its resources. In the present context, the awareness among the University teachers is studied, based on the services offered by a typical Indian University Library. At the same time, awareness of library services influences the library visits of a library clientele. As such the study is also intended to find out the frequency of visits made to the University Library by the teachers.

Awareness of Library Services

The Library services offered by a University Library generally include:

(1) Reference Service (RS),

(2) Bibliographical Service (BS),

(3) Current Awareness Service (CAS),

(4) Selective Dissimination of Information (SDI),

(5) Inter-Library Loan (ILL),

(6) Reprography (REP) and

(7) Translation Service (TS).

Chi-square technique was employed to study the significance of awareness of University Library services among the University teachers by framing the following null hypothesis.

H_0 : The number of teachers is the same with respect to each of the library services known to them.

If this hypothesis is true, one can expect an equal number of cases under each factor, as shown in Table 8.3.

Table 8.3
Awareness of Library Services Among the University Teachers

	No. of Teachers Aware of the Library Services							
	RS	*BS*	*CAS*	*SDI*	*ILL*	*REP*	*TS*	*Total*
Observed values	136	76	80	53	30	97	39	511
Expected values	73	73	73	73	73	73	73	

Source : Computed from the Survey Data.

The calculated chi-square value 109.66 is greater than the critical value (12.59) with six degrees of freedom at 0.05 level of significance.

It can be decuced that there is unequal awareness of library services among the University teachers.

As such cadre-wise awareness of library services was studied by analysing the data further, which is shown in Table 8.4.

Table 8.4
Cadre-wise Awareness of Library Services

Services	*Awareness Among Teachers*			*Total Aggregate Irrespective of the Cadres*
	Professors	*Readers*	*Lecturers*	
Reference Service	21 (72.41)	50 (86.2)	65 (90.27)	136 (85.53)
Bibliographical Service	12 (41.37)	24 (41.37)	40 (55.55)	76 (47.79)
CAS	12 (41.37)	29 (50.00)	39 (54.16)	80 (50.31)
SDI	5 (17.24)	19 (32.75)	29 (40.27)	53 (33.33)
Inter-Library Loan	4 (13.79)	12 (20.68)	14 (19.44)	30 (18.86)
Reprography	14 (48.27)	31 (53.44)	52 (72.22)	97 (61.0)
Translation	8 (27.58)	16 (27.58)	15 (20.83)	39 (24.52)

Figure in the parentheses indicate the percentages.

Source : Calculated from the Survey Data.

The data from Table 8.4 demonstrates that 'Reference service' has the highest awareness among 85.53 percent of the teachers who have acknowledged it. 'Reprography' is the next service of which 61 percent of the teachers are aware. Awareness of 'Current Awareness Service' is seen among 50.31 percent of the teaching community, thus occupying the third position. This is followed by 'Bibliographical Service' with awareness among 47.79 percent of the teachers. Further, it is found that 'Selective Dissemination of Information', Inter-Library Loan' and 'Translation Service' are known to about 19 to 34 percent of the teachers.

Among Professors 72.41 percent are well aware of the 'Reference Service' and 48.27 percent about 'Reprography'.

Readers are also found aware of 'Reference Service' (86.2 percent) followed by 'Current Awareness Service' (50 percent) and 'Reprography' (53 percent).

Among Lecturers, 90.27 percent and 72.22 percent are aware of 'Reference Service' and 'Reprography' respectively. About 56 percent of the Lecturers are aware of 'Bibliographical Service' and 54 percent 'Current Awareness Service'.

The following services are found widely aware of among the teacher based on 50 percent as the cut-off point in the aggregate percentage. They are :

(*a*) Reference Service,

(*b*) Reprography, and

(*c*) Current Awareness Service.

Visits to the University Library

The frequency of visits of the University Library among the teachers was studied by using the chi-square technique, by framing the following null hypothesis.

H_0 : The frequency of visits to University Library is same among all teachers.

If this hypothesis is true one can expect an equal number of cases under each factor. This is indicated in Table 8.5.

Table 8.5
Teachers Visiting University Library

Frequency of visits	Observed values	Expected values
Everyday	26	26.5
Thrice a week	36	26.5
Twice a week	40	26.5
Once a week	37	26.5
Once a fortnight	13	26.5
Once a month	7	26.5
Total	159	

Source : Computed from the Survey Data.

group among the University teachers are found less aware of library services and use the Library lesser than that of their junior teachers.

Time Spent in Reading and Consulting Documents among the University Teachers

To find out the time spent in reading, hours per week are taken as a unit. Table 8.7 shows the number of hours spent by teachers per week in reading and referring books for collecting information. The time spent is divided into two groups, namely "less than fifteen hours" and "fifteen hours and above".

The figures in Table 8.7 point out that about 82 percent of the teachers irrespective of their cadre spend below 15 hours of their reading time in a week in the University Library whereas about 60 percent less than fifteen hours at home and in the department. The percentage of teachers who spend time in consulting books in the State Regional Library is however only 3 percent.

On the other side, about 16 percent of Lecturers, irrespective of the reading place, are spending at least fifteen hours per week, which has a notable difference when compared to that of Professors and Readers. A high percentage (42) of teachers irrespective of their cadre spend cadre spend less than fifteen hours in reading or consulting books.

Further analysis of figures shows that on the whole Lecturers spend more time in referring books and they are followed by Professors and Readers having lower level of creativity spend more time in consulting documents.

Time Spent in Reading—School-wise

Time spent in reading documents at various places by the University teachers was studied school-wise and the same was presented in Table 8.8.

Table 8.7
Time Spent in Reading by the University Teachers at Various Places

Place of Reading	Time spent in hours per week (cadre-wise)						Aggregate figures (irrespective of the Cadres)	
	Professors		Readers		Lecturers			
	<15	>15	<15	>15	<15	>15	<15	> 15
At home	16 (55.17)	11 (37.93)	38 (65.51)	18 (31.03)	45 (62.50)	24 (33.33)	99 (61.06)	53 (34.09)
In the Department	20 (68.96)	9 (31.03)	33 (56.89)	20 (34.48)	43 (59.72)	26 (36.11)	96 (61.85)	55 (33.87)
In the University main Library	23	0	46 (79.31)	2 (3.44)	62 (86.11)	8 (11.11)	131 (81.57)	10 (4.85)
In the State Regional Library	1 (3.44)	0	3 (5.17)	0	1 (1.38)	0	5 (3.33)	0
Other Places	1 (3.44)	0	0	0	1 (1.38)	0	2 (1.60)	0
Aggregate figures irrespective of the place (in percent)	42.06	13.79	41.38	13.78	42.21	16.11	41.88	14.56

N.B < indicates less than;

> indicates greater than.

Figures in the parentheses indicate percentages

Source: Computed from the survey data.

Table 8.8
Time Spent in Reading at Various Places (School-wise)

Place of Reading	Time spent in hours per week by teachers (School-wise)										Aggregate Figure (Irrespective of School)	
	SBES		SHES		SMPS		SSBS		SBM			
	<15	>15	<15	>15	<15	>15	<15	> 15	<15	>15	<15	>15
At home	22 (73.3)	8 (26.6)	26 (60.4)	14 (32.5)	20 (66.6)	10 (33.3)	28 (57.1)	18 (36.7)	3 (42.8)	3 (42.8)	99 (60.04)	53 (34.38)
In the Department	16 (53.3)	14 (46.6)	29 (67.4)	12 (27.9)	20 (66.6)	9 (30.0)	27 (55.1)	18 (36.7)	4 (57.1)	2 (28.5)	96 (59.9)	55 (33.94)
In the University main library	26 (86.6)	1 (3.3)	36 (83.7)	3 (6.9)	26 (86.6)	0	37 (75.5)	6 (12.3)	6 (85.7)	0	131 (83.62)	10 (4.48)
In the State Regional Library	2 (6.6)	–	3 '(6.9)	–	–	–	–	–	–	–	5 (2.7)	–
Other Places	1 (3.3)	–	–	–	–	–	1 (2.0)	–	–		2 (1.06)	–
Aggregate figures irrespective of the place in percent	44.62	15.3	43.68	13.46	43.96	12.66	37.94	17.12	37.12	14.26	41.46	14.56

N.B <indicates less than; > indicates greater than

Figures in the parentheses indicate percentages.
Source: Computed from the survey data.

It is evident from Table 8.8 that more teachers (above 65 percent) from SBES and SMPS spend 'less than fifteen hours, per week at home than the teachers from the other two schools SSBS and SHES. Comparatively teachers from these two schools and Business Management spend more than fifteen hours per week at home. Interestingly, among all schools, more number of teachers (about 67 percent) from SHES spend 'less than fifteen hours' per week in the department. However, a high percentage of (30 percent and above) science teachers spend 'more than fifteen hours' of time per week in the departments is compared to that of the teachers of Humanities and Social Sciences. Significantly, a high percentage of social science teachers are found spending more than fifteen hours of time per week in the University Library.

As a whole irrespective of the place of reading it is observed that science teachers spend more time in reading and referring documents than that of teachers of Humanities and Social Sciences.

Time spent in reading and consulting documents at selective places by the University teachers irrespective of cadre was also studied (Table 8.9).

Table 8.9
Time Spent in Reading at Selective Places

Place of Reading	*No. of Teachers Who Spent Time (hours per week)*						*Total Percentage*
	< 15			*>15*			
	Percentage	*Fo*	*Fe*	*Fo*	*Fe*		
At home	62.26	99	(111.6)	53	(40.39)	33.33	152 (95.5)
Department	60.37	96	(110.86)	55	(40.13)	34.59	151 (94.9)
University Library	82.38	141	(103.52)	10	(37.47)	6.28	141 (94.9)
Grand Total :		336		118			444

N..B.: < indicates less than;
> indicates more than.

Figures in the parentheses indicate expected values.

Source : Computed from the Survey Data.

To see the statistical significance of the results in Table 8.9 the following null hypothesis was framed.

H_0 : Time spent in reading and the place of reading among University teachers with respect to information gathering are independent attributes.

The independence of the attributes was tested with chi-square test using the data. The value of chi-square 40.2947, which is very high compared to the critical value (5.99) with two degrees of freedom at 0.05 level of significance. As such the hypothesis of independence cannot be accepted. The conclusion is that the time spent in reading among the University teachers is closely related to the place of reading for gathering information.

Among teachers irrespective of cadre 95.5 percent spend their reading time at home, 94.9 percent in the Department and 88.6 percent in the University Library respectively.

Reasons for Seeking Information

Reasons for seeking information are the factors directly influencing the information needs. As such the information needs of the University teaching community include :

1. Classroom work,
2. Awareness of new knowledge,
3. Participation in seminars/conferences,
4. To meet the needs of promotional opportunities,
5. Generate new information,
6. Writing of text books, etc.

To study these reasons among the University teachers priority type questions were framed in the questionnaire. The responses were analysed by using points for each rank viz., 1st rank was given for 7 points, 2nd rank for 6 points, 3rd rank for 5 points. Like this 7th rank for 1 point. Thus, the responses were analysed and presented in Table 8.10.

Table 8.10
Reasons for Seeking Information

Sl. No.	*Reasons*	*Points and Ranks Among*			*Total Points and Ranks*
		Professors	*Readers*	*Lecturers*	
1.	To prepare for class room	160 (1)	348 (1)	421 (1)	929 (1)
2.	General awareness of new knowledge	158 (2)	297 (2)	387 (2)	842 (2)
3.	For participating in the Seminars/ Conferences, etc.	112 (3)	251 (3)	289 (3)	652 (3)
4.	To meet the needs of promotional opportunities	54 (5)	116 (6)	197 (5)	367 (5)
5.	To generate new information out of curiosity and inquisitiveness	94 (4)	171 (4)	288 (4)	553 (4)
6.	To write text-books	51 (6)	137 (5)	132 (6)	320 (6)
7.	Other reasons : Like research work etc.	21 (7)	36 (7)	40 (7)	97 (7)

Figures in the parentheses indicate ranks.

Source : Computed from the Survey Data.

From Table 8.10 it may be understood that primarily, teachers irrespective of their cadre, collected information in the preparation of their day-to-day teaching work. Information collected for general thirst for new knowledge is found as secondary nature. Participation in seminars/conferences, etc., occupied the third place and to generate new information out of curiosity and inquisitiveness was claimed as fourth reason in gathering information. Information sought to meet the promotional opportunities was considered as the fifth cause. Information gathered with the purpose of writing text books and other reasons occupied the sixth and seventh positions respectively.

Suggestions Received on University Library Services

The teachers were asked to offer their suggestions for the University Library services. The suggestions included like modifications to the existing services, acquisition of documents, attitudes of the library staff towards the visitors etc. To put them in an order, they are grouped into : general services, documentation services, arrangement of documents on shelves and procurement of documents and suggestions relating to the attitude of the library staff.

A. General Services include the following :

(*a*) Need for strengthening the inter-library loan service;

(*b*) Reprographic should be made available uninterruptedly;

(*c*) Strengthening of the departmental libraries by developing collection and maintaining separate catalogues for each department;

(*d*) Issue of books on all working days i.e., including Sundays, Second Saturdays and also on holidays when the Library is kept opened for reference and study;

(*e*) Need to extend the timings of the counter transactions;

(*f*) Reducing the period for returning books of teaching faculty instead of one year;

(*g*) There is need for quickening the counter services;

(*h*) Need for exhibiting on boards the services offered by the Library, which brings awareness among the users; and

(*i*) Need for library orientation programmes for better utilization of library services.

B. 'Documentation Services' comprise the following :

(*a*) Need for establishing documentation centre to cater the information needs of teachers and research scholars.

(*b*) The present current awareness service is not adequate. There is need to modify and expand the services.

(*c*) The bibliographical services are awfully insufficient. Something should be done to improve the services.

C. 'Organization of books' consist the following points of suggestions :

(*a*) There is the need to check the misplacement of books on shelves.

(*b*) There is the need for proper display of recent books and journals in the Library.

(*c*) Many of the books pertaining to the subjects like Tamil, Urdu, Persian, Hindi and Sanskrit are not classified. There is high felt need to classify and catalogue them and arrange them in a systematic way for proper utilization of these subject books.

(*d*) Books in the binding section need to be arranged in (a systematic way) an order making easy to pick up a required book.

D. 'Procurement of documents' include the following

(*a*) Non-availability of subject periodicals is hampering the academic activities to a greater extent. Most of the teachers have expressed that something should be done in this regard to improve the collection of journals.

(*b*) Need of procuring latest text books of foreign editions.

(*c*) There is the need to improve the collection of reference books.

(*d*) Arrangements should also be made for obtaining abstracts at free of cost from the concerned centres.

(*e*) Need of obtaining Ph.D. copies of foreign countries.

(*f*) Inordinate delay in procuring books should be avoided.

(*g*) Need to increase and strengthen the library funds fo purchasing books and journals.

E. With regard to 'Attitude of the Library Staff' the following two suggestions were offered :

(*a*) Need for prompt service from the library staff in locating the books. Attitude of professionals in reference service is questioned by the teachers.

(*b*) The library staff are habituated to talk loudly and hence, there is need for strict silence in the Library.

CHAPTER 9

SUMMARY, CONCLUSIONS, FINDINGS AND SUGGESTIONS

Summary

Information production is a cyclic process starting from generation phase, when recorded it becomes a source which is reused, sometimes even by the creator giving rise to new information. Information is not only dynamic in the sense of constant transfer, but also in the sense of continuous evolution. Information is constantly evolving, even with respect to communication within one person.

Information is a significant element in the development of human society, having immense economic and social value. It is vital to the proper functioning of a democratic society. It may be in many forms viz., news, facts, statistics, reports, legislation, tax codes, judicial decisions, resolutions and the like. The quantity of information required for taking decisions vary from person to person depending on the situation, speed at which decision is taken and the place at which decision is taken.

The increasing need and dependence on information, the increase in technological sophistication and the complexities of modern social life have increased its nature and value. It is said that the nature and value of information is directly related to its communication. Information is a social process, as its nature and value are closely related to the information needs and approaches for information by the individuals. In this context, the concept of information is more complex as it is associated with variables such as 'nascent', 'reliable', 'cost', 'value' etc. It is a direct input to the process of generation of new information, decision-making, and deriving emotional satisfaction, Indirectly, it is an input to the process of production of commodities and services. It is an energy resource intended to initiate desired actions.

Whether we call it information production or information creation or creativity, the act is confined relatively to a small portion of world's population, who could device new methods, reorganise existing ideas and offer improved solutions to the familiar problems. They create new horizons and set new standards in science, technology, literature, fine arts, business, industry and social leadership.

Universities bear the responsibility of building these people called society of elites, needed for a prosperous nation. The elite group thus built includes scientists, engineers, economists, medical professionals, lawyers, etc., who have the nature of free thinking, self realization, sharing the responsibility for the uplift of the society, One of the main goals of the universities is developing of new ideas and ways of doing things that are appropriate to the changing circumstances of society. In this direction, University teachers are involved in research activities, publication of articles in journals and text-books, preparation and revision of curricula of advanced studies, etc., in addition to transmission of knowledge to improve the quality of life in the society.

Information generation is the outcome of interaction between the problems and their solutions. It is solely connected with the intelligence and thinking of the individuals. Hence, the impact of the surroundings play a key role on the individual. The people involved in information generation are influenced by social factors (viz., information exchange between individuals and groups of individuals), family (its size and dependents), age and sex. The personality characteristics such as intelligence, awareness, flexibility and originality also influence the creativity.

Information generation, information source is the fundamental unit. It is fundamental because it cannot be broken down without destroying the information. If it is to be reused, the information sources need to be verified, edited, enhanced with a table of contents and index, and physically stored at a place. This provides continuous access to information sources and results in the establishment of information resources. These information resources include libraries, information centres, invisible colleges, information exchange groups, etc. These may be grouped into active resources and passive resources. The use of passive resources viz., libraries, information centres largely depend on the initiative and efforts of users.[1]

The vital ingredient of the university system, the teacher, is the subject of the present study. The study is aimed at evaluating the performance of the teacher in information generation against cadre, service, sex and influence of helpful and unhelpful factors. The relations between the information generation and the awareness of library services and their use are also studied.

The sample was selected from the population of teaching community working in S.V. University College of Arts and Sciences, Tirupati, by employing Stratified Random Sampling technique. The sample included all the three cadres—Professors, Readers and Lecturers and it was slightly higher than 50 percent of the population. Data was collected through the well designed questionnaire, after conducting a pilot study. The analysis of data has yielded the following conclusions.

Conclusions

Following are the conclusions drawn from this study in relation with the framed hypotheses :

1. Information generation by the University teachers is not same among all cadres. Gradual increase in information generation is observed from Lecturer cadre to Professor cadre (Hypothesis-1)

2. Information generation by the University teachers steadily increased to certain years of service and from there it decreased (Hypothesis-2)

3. The factors sex and cadre are related and play a key role in information generation (Hypothesis-3).

4. 'Healthy atmosphere in the faculty' is the predominant helpful factor among the 'Faculty Environment Factors' for generating information by the University teachers (Hypothesis-4)

5. It is found that 'Financial Assistance' as a helpful factor has no significant impact on information generation by the University teachers (Hypothesis-5).

6. 'Recognition of the work' is claimed by a majority of the Lecturers indicating psychological dissatisfaction among younger generation with regard to recognition of the work done by them (Hypothesis-6).

7. Visits of friends and relatives, health problems of the family members and personal health; education of the dependents; and size of the family, are predominant unhelpful domestic factors coming in the way of information generation by the University teachers (Hypothesis-7).

8. Burden of the workload due to teaching activity, research guidance, problems with colleagues and officials are the vital unhelpful academic and official factors hampering information generation by the University teachers (Hypothesis-8).

9. From the study it is found that university teachers mainly depend on University Library, its resources and its services for seeking information (Hypothesis-9).

10. It is found that there is no relation between the cadre of the University teachers and the awareness of library service and usage (Hypothesis-10).

11. Information generation is not directly proportionate to the time spent in reading by a University teacher (Hypothesis-11).

Findings

In addition to the conclusions inferred, the following findings were found during the course of the study.

It is observed that information generation Professors are more consistent than Readers and Lecturers. Interestingly, the inconsistency is high among Readers as compared to that of Lecturers.

Data on cadre-wise generation of information of a person was not forthcoming. As many of the respondents were not filling this aspect they were personally approached and information was sought. They felt that it was difficult for them to provide the information cadre-wise.

Information Generation Index (IGI) never increased but rather decreased steeply as service increased in the case of those who remained as Lecturers. It is observed that whatever creativity that could be achieved was done within 10 years as Lecturers, and it did not increase when they remained as Lecturers at the time of investigation. This might be due to the fact that if once frustration sets in, the Lecturers were not inclined to be productive any more afterwards.

Further, it is found that the service group of 11-20 years has a lot of bearing for better information generation and the effect of more when a cadre benefit is given during such service range.

Female teachers were found performing better in generating information before they because Readers. There is no further increase in information generation in the Reader cadre.

In the course of the study it is found that majority of the teachers are found being inspired by professional colleagues and friends for generating new information rather than by documents.

With regard to use of agencies for information, though teachers (96.8 percent) mainly depended on University Library resources and services; the use of 'Personal Collection of documents' by 72 percent of the teachers indicates its importance next to the University Library. Among the teachers about 60 percent made use of 'Departmental Libraries' and 'off-prints' obtained from authors for collecting information.

It is discovered that as a whole 50 percent of teachers are widely aware of 'Reference Service', 'Reprography' and 'Current Awareness Service' among the services offered by the University Library.

In case of visits of the University Library it is noticed that 'twice a week' is the model frequency among teachers irrespective of their cadre. Cadre-wise among Professors it is 'once a week', and in respect of Readers and Lecturers it is 'twice a week' and 'everyday' respectively.

Further, it is learnt that irrespective of the place of reading, science teachers spend more time in reading and referring documents than the teachers of Humanities and Social Sciences. On comparison between the time spent in reading and the place of reading (viz., home, department and university library), it is found that there is a close relation between the time spent in reading and the place of reading.

The University Library, its collection and services can also be taken as one of the helpful factors having impact on information generation. Because information generation is based on the timely supply and accuracy of the information supplied by the Library, the opinions offered by the respondents on the University Library, organization of its collection, and services offered, etc. have great importance in finding its role as one of the helpful factors.

Among teachers 22 percent have expressed that something should be done to improve the inter-library loan service, reprographic service, counter services and library orientation programmes.

About 12 percent of the teachers have felt the need of establishing a separate documentation centre to overcome the inadequate current awareness service and bibliographical services offered by the University Library.

About 15.7 percent of the teachers expressed that books were misplaced and journals and recent additions of books were not properly displayed. They further expressed that most of the books pertaining to language, i.e., English and Telugu, were not properly classified and catalogued and thus leading to difficult situation in locating the required books.

About 32 percent of teachers felt the need to increase library funds to procure sufficient number of books and journals, as the non-availability to subject journals is coming in the way of their academic activity.

Non-availability of prompt reference service from the library professionals on approach, was also felt by some of the teachers.

On the basis of the aforementioned opinions expressed by the teachers, the extent of the use of University Library as a helpful factor in information generation is assessed and it is learnt that there is need to improve the existing services and to introduce new ones to suit the information needs of the teachers.

Suggestions

From the investigation it is found that the University Library is used as a main agency of information by the university teachers. Taking into account their opinions on S.V. University Library services and organization of collection, the following suggestions are put forward for consideration for improvement of the standards of its performance and increase of information generation in a better manner to satisfy the requirements of the university academic community.

1. To improve the standards of the University, there is the need to bring out some new reforms in the selection policy of the persons to the faculty. As is the case in Western countries and in the United States of America in particular, the selection of the faculty members should have— (*a*) persons solely connected with teaching, and (*b*) persons exclusively meant to perform research. This type of selection will lessen the work-load among them and lead to better performance in their career.

2. In the present system, research guidance leading to M. Phils. and Ph.Ds. and taking up of research projects may be left to the second category of persons and transmission of knowledge to the first category of persons as mentioned above. This kind of bifurcation among the faculty avoids the clash between teaching and research activity, thereby giving ample time and energy for better performance.

3. Establishment of 'User Service Unit' in the University Library under the supervision of an experienced professional not below the rank of Deputy Librarian /Documentation Officer, to offer services to the library users, viz., preparation documentation lists on demand or in anticipation. Current Awareness Service and inter-library loan service is yet another suggestion that may be considered. With the cooperation of other University Libraries in Andhra Pradesh union catalogue of journal may be prepared for better resource sharing. This service can be improved by preparing content pages of various journals subject-wise for the benefit of teachers and research scholars.

4. A reference library may be established in the main building of the University Colleges of Arts and Science on the lines of Book Bank of S.V. University College of Engineering, to meet the immediate information needs of teachers and researchers.

5. For better organisation of library collections and to check the misplacements of books and journals, all the professional assistants, excepting those connected with circulation section and reprography, may be drafted to work for one hour. Each one may be alloted a particular area in the stocks to check the collection. This will certainly improve the arrangement of the documents in the shelves.

6. To improve the professional ethics among the library staff, refresher courses may be conducted in the University itself or staff may be deputed to undergo such courses in other

universities or institutions. Further, the Library staff may be motivated by giving additional increments for additional qualification or by promotion to higher positions.

Areas for Further Research

In the process of the investigation, the following areas are found suitable for further research in the University—

(*i*) Information generation by the University teachers prior to and after marriage in their career.

(*ii*) Information generation by the University teachers studied individually throughout their service in various cadres can be related with 'logistic curve'

(*iii*) Relation between age (at various intervals viz., 30 years, 35 years, 40 years etc.) and information generated by the University teachers can be a theme for an investigation.

Studies leading to the evaluation of performance of the University teaching community are scarcely seen in Indian context. At a time when the standards of universities and teachers' performance are criticised, it can be stated that studies of present nature occupy a unique position in the research in general and 'library and information science' in particular.

BIBLIOGRAPHY

Abraham, Alexander and Karisiddappa, C.R. : A Survey of Library Service Rendered to Science Research Scholars by the Calicut University, *Lucknow Librarian,* 18(3), 1986, pp. 90-95.

Ackoff, R.L. and Vergara, E.: Creativity in Problem Solving and Planning: A Review, *European Journal of Operational Research,* 7, 1981, pp. 1-13.

Adiseshaiah, Malcolm S.: Role of Universities as Agents of Change . In veera Raghavan, J. (Ed.) : Higher Education in the Eighties Opportunities and Objectives. New Delhi : Lancer International, 1985.

Adolf Butenandt, H.C.: The Role of Research and the Problems Involved in Promoting It, *Universitas,* 15(1), 1973, pp. 1-12.

Allen, T.J.: Information Needs and Uses, *Annual Review of Information Science and Technology,* 4 1969, pp. 3-29.

Allen, T.J.: and Gertsberger, P.G.: Criteria for Selection of An Information Source,. *Journal of Applied Psychology,* 52(4), 1968, pp. 272-279.

Alpaugh, P.K. and Birren, James E.: Are There Sex Differences in Creativity Across the Adult Life Span ? *Human Development,* 18(6), 1975, pp. 461-465.

American Institute of Physics : A Program For a National Information System For Physics and Astronomy 1971-75., Information Division, American Institute of Physics, 1970.

American Psychological Association : Reports of the American Psychological Association's Project on Scientific Information Exchange in Psychology., Vol.2, Reports 10-15 (Study 10), 1965.

Andrus, R.R. : Approach to Information Evaluation., *M.S.U. Business Topics,* Summer, 1971, pp. 40-45.

Artandi, Susan : Information Concepts And Their Utility., *Journal of the American Society for Information Science,* 24, 1973, pp. 242-245.

Artandi, Susan : Man, Information and Society : New Patterns of Interaction, *Journal of the American Society for Information Science,* January, 1979, pp. 15-18.

Austin, J.H.: Chase, Chance and Creativity, Columbia : Columbia University Press, 1978.

Balu, Peter M.: The Organization of Academic Work., New York : John Wiley and Sons, 1973.

Barchillon, J.: Creativity and its Inhibition in Child Prodigies : Personality Dimensions of Creativity., New York : Lincoln Institute of Psycho-therapy, 1961.

Barrington, E.J.W.: The Importance of Information For Creative Biological Research., *Information Service and Use,* 3, (1983) pp. 23-33.

Barron, Frank : Creativity and Psychological Health, Princeton, N.J.: Van Nostrand, 1963.

Bawden, David.: Information System And the Stimulation of Creativity., *Journal of Information Science,* 12, 1986, pp. 203-216.

Bernal, J.D.: Report on the Royal Society Scientific Information Conference., Royal Society, 1948.

Beveridge, W.J.B.: Seeds of Discovery., London : Hienemann, 1980.

Bhattacharya, G.: Information Sciences : A Unified View Through A Systems Approach, IASLIC, 1978.

Bell, D.: Social Framework of Information Theory. *In :* Dertouzos, M.L. and Mosses (Ed): The Computer Age, A Twenty Year View, Cambridge : MIT Press, 1979.

Biggs, M.: Sources of Tension and Conflict between Librarians and Faculty, *Journal of Higher Education*, 52, 1981, pp. 180-201.

Bose, Nirmal Kumar : Universities and Research. *In :* Shah, A.B. (Ed.): Higher Education in India. Bombay : Lalvani Publishing House, 1967.

Brady, E.L. and Branscomb, L.M.: Information in a Changing Society., *Science*, 175, 1972, pp. 961-966.

Braman, S.: Defining Information,. *Telecommunications Policy*, 13, 1989, pp. 233-242.

Brittain, J.M.: Information And Its Users : A Review With Special Reference to Social Sciences, New York : Wiley - Inter Science, 1970.

Brittain, J.M.: Information Services and Knowledge Creation in the Social Sciences, *ICSSR Newsletter*, January-March, 1987, pp. 17-33.

Bronowski, J.: The Creative Process, *Scientific American*, 199(3), 1958, pp. 58-66.

Brookers, B.C.: Foundations of Information Science, *Journal of Information Science*, 2(3-4), 1980, pp. 125-133.

Burchard, J.E.: How Humanists Use A Library. *In :* Overcharge, C.F.J. and Harman, J.R. (Eds.): Intrex : Report on Planning Conference And Information Transfer Experiments, September 3, 1965., Cambridge, Mass : M.I.T. Press, 1965.

Buckland, Michael K.: Information as Thing., *Journal of the American Society for Information Science*, 42(5), 1991, pp. 351-360.

Carroll, Bonnie C. and King, Donal W.: Value of Information, *Drexel Library Quarterly,* 21(3), 1985, pp. 39-60.

Caston, Geoffrey : Conflicts Within University Community, *Studies in Higher Education,* 2(1), 1977, pp. 3-8.

Cattel, R.W. and Drevdahl, J.E.A.: A Comparison of the Personality Profile (16 PF) of Eminent Researchers with that of Eminent Teachers and Administrators and of the General Population, *British Journal of Psychology,* 46, 1955, pp. 248-261.

Chen, C. and Hernon, P.: Information Seeking : Assessing and Anticipating User Needs, New York : Neal-Schuman, 1982.

Chen, C.C.: How Do Scientists Meet Their Information Needs ? *Special Libraries,* 65, July 1974, pp. 272-280.

Cole, J.R. and Cole, S.: Social Stratification in Science, Chicago : Chicago University Press, 1973.

Crane, D.: Collaboration : Communication and Influence, A Study of the Effects of Formal and Informal Collaboration Among Scientists, John Hopkins University, 1968.

Crane, D.: Information Needs and Uses, *Annual Review of Information Science and Technology,* 6, 1971, pp. 3-39.

Crane, D.: Invisible Colleges : Diffusion of Knowledge in Scientific Communities, Chicago : University of Chicago Press, 1972.

Crawford, S.: Information Needs and Uses, *Annual Review of Information Science and Technology,* 13, 1978, pp. 61-81.

Cronin, Blaise : Assessing User Needs, *Aslib Proceedings,* 33, 1981, pp. 37-47.

Daniel, Evelyn : Information Resources and Organisational Structure, *Journal of the American Society for Information Science,* 34(3), 1983, pp. 222-228.

Davis, G.B.: Management Information Systems, New York : McGraw Hill, 1974.

De Bono, E.: Lateral Thinking : A Textbook of Creativity, London : Ward Lock, 1970.

Debons, A. (ed.): Information Science : Search for Unity, New York : Marcel Dekker, 1974.

De Haan, R.F. and Havighurst, R.J.: Educating Gifted Children, Chicago : University of Chicago Press, 1961.

Dennis, Wayne : Productivity Among American Psychologists, *American Psychologists,* 9, 1954, pp. 191-194.

Derr, Richard L.: Information Seeking Expressions of Users, *Journal of the American Society for Information Science*, 35(2), 1984, pp. 124-128.

Dervin, B.: Strategies For Dealing With Human Information Needs : Information or Communication. *Journal of Broadcasting,* 20, 1976, pp. 324-333.

Dervin, B. et. al.: Measuring Aspects of Information Seeking : A Test of A Quantitative/Qualitative Methodology. *In* : Communication Year Book, 6, California, Sage : Beverly Hills, 1982, pp. 419-444.

De Sola Pool, I.: Tracking the Flow of Information,. *Science,* (4611), 1983, pp. 609-613.

De Solla Price, D.J.: Little Science : Big Science, New York : Columbia University Press, 1963.

Dewing, Kathuleen : Family Influence On Creativity, *Journal of Special Education,* 4(4), 1970, pp. 399-404.

Doucet, J.: Information and Creativity, *Impact of Science on Society,* 1979, pp. 394-395.

Dretske, F.I.: Knowledge and the Flow of Information, Cambridge, Massachusetts : M.I.T. Press. 1981.

Drucker, P.F.: The Age of Discontinuity : Guidelines To Our Changing Society, New York : Harper and Row, 1969.

Eiduson, B.T.: Scientists : Their Psychological World, New York : Basic Books, 1962.

Ennis, P.H.: The Study of Use and Users of Recorded Knowledge, *Library Quarterly,* 34(Oct.), 1964, pp. 305-314.

Faibisoff, S.G. and Ely, D.P.: Information and Information Needs, *Information Reports and Bibliographies,* 5, 1976, pp. 2-16.

Fairthrone, R.A.: Information : One Lable, Several Bottles. *In* : Debons, Anthony and Camerom, William J. (Ed.): Perspectives in Information Science, Leyden : Noordhoff International Publishing, 1975, pp. 65-73.

Fairthrone, R.A.: Morphology of Information Flow, *Journal of Association for Computing Machinery,* 14, 1967, pp. 710-719.

Farradane, J.: The Nature of Information, *Journal of Information Science,* 1(1), 1979, pp. 13-17.

Fjallbrant, Nancy : Planning A Programme of Library User Education, *Journal of Librarianship,* 9(3), 1977, pp. 199-211.

Flower, B.H.: Survey of Information Needs of Physicists and Chemists, *Journal of Documentation,* 21(2), June 1965, pp. 83-112.

Ford, N.: Knowledge Structures in Human and Machine Information Processing—Their Representation and Interaction, *Social Science Information Studies,* Vol. 3, 1983, pp. 209-222.

Foskett, D.J.: Pathways for Communication, London : Bingley, 1983.

Foster, John : Creativity and The Teacher, London : Macmillan, 1971.

Freud, Sigmund : Creative Writers and Day-dreaming. London : The Hogarth Press and the Institute of Psycho-Analysis, 1959, Vol. 9.

Garfield, E.: A Tribute to Ranganathan, *Current Contents,* 6, 1984, pp. 3-10.

Garvey, W.D. et. al.: Communication in the Physical and Social Sciences: The Process of Dissemination and Assimilating Information Differ in These Two groups of Sciences, *Science*, 170 (3963), 1970, pp. 1166-1173.

Ghiselin, Brewster (Ed.) : The Creative Process. Berkely, California University of California Press, 1952.

Goffman, W.: Information Science : Discipline or Disappearance, *ASLIB Proceedings*, 22(12), 1970, pp. 589-596.

Grogan, Denis : Science and Technology, An Introduction to the Literature, London : Bingley, 1976.

Gross, Edward and Grambsch, Paul V.: Changes in University Organization 1964-1971, New York : McGraw-Hill, 1974.

Gruber, Howard E. et al., (Eds.): Contemporary Approaches to Creative Thinking, New York : Prentice Hall, 1962.

Guilford, J.P.: Factors that aid and hinder creativity *Teachers College Record*, 65, 1962, pp. 380-392.

Guilford, J.P.: The Nature of Human Intelligence, London : Mcgraw-Hill, 1967.

Gupta, B.M.: Information Communication and Technology Transfer : A Review of Literature, *Annals of Library Science and Documentation*, 28(1-4), 1981, pp. 1-13.

Hall, J.: Information Services in University Libraries, *Aslib Proceedings*, 24(5), 1972, pp. 293-302.

Hallman, Ralph J.: The Necessary and Sufficient Conditions of Creativity, *Journal of Humanistic Psychology*, 3, Spring, 1963, pp. 14-27.

Halloran, James D.: Information and Communication, *Aslib Proceedings*, 31(1), 1979, pp. 21-28.

Hanson, C.W.: Introduction to Science-Information Work, London : Aslib, 1971.

Hatchard, Dermond B. and Toy, Phyllis : The Psychological Barriers between Library Users and Library Staff : An Exploratory Investigation, *Australian Academic and Research Libraries,* 17(2), 1986, pp. 63-69.

Hayes, R.M.: Information is Librarianship, *Libri,* 19(3), 1969. pp. 216-236.

Hayes, R.M. and Becker, J.: Hand Book of Data Processing for Libraries,. New York : Wiley, 1970.

Hommadi, Ahmed Hussain : University Administration in Developing Countries., Delhi : Indian Bibliographies Bureau, 1984.

Hoong, Yip Yat (Ed.): Role of Universities in National Development Planning in South-east Asia : Proceedings of the Workshop held in Singapore, 26-29 July, 1971, Singapore : RIHED, 1971.

Horne, E.E.: Question Generation and Formulation : An Indication of Information Need, *Journal of the American Society for Information Science,* 34(1), 1983, pp. 5-15.

Hovde, Frederick L : The University and National Strength. *In* : University. Madras : Higginbothams Private Ltd., 1968

Jayalakshmi Indiresan : Faculty Development : Some Issues and Trends, *University News,* 29(2), 1991, pp. 29-34.

Jencks, C. and Riesman, D.: The Academic Revolution, New York : Doubleday, 1968.

John, V.V.: Universities and Research. *In* : Shah, A.B. (Ed.): Higher Education in Indial, Bombay : Lalvani, 1967.

Kasperson, C.J.: An Analysis of the Relationship Between Information Sources and Creativity in Scientists and Engineers., *Human Communication Research,* 4, 1978, pp. 113-119.

Kaysen, Carl : The Higher Learning : The Universities and the Public, Princeton, New Jersey : Princeton University Press, 1969.

Kent, A.K.: Information As Power, *ASLIB Proceedings,* 31(1), 1979, pp. 16-20.

Kerawalla, G.J.: The Role of the Teacher : Changing Perspectives, *University News,* 29(2), 1991, pp. 25-28.

Kerr, Clark : The Uses of the University, Cambridge, Mass : Harvard University Press, 1963.

Khanna, J.K.: Communicating Knowledge : Gateway to Knowledge, Kurukshetra : Research Publications.

Kneller, George F.: The Art and Science of Creativity, New York : Holt, Rinehart and Winston, 1965.

Koblitz, L.: Librarianship and Documentation/Information : Distinctive Features and Common Aspects. *In :* On Theoretical Problems in Informatics, Moscow : All-Union Institute for Scientific and Technical Information, 1969.

Kochen, Manfred : Information Science Research : The Search for the Nature of Information, *Journal of the American Society for - Information Science,* 35(3), 1984, pp. 194-199.

Kochen Manfred : Stability in the Growth of Knowledge, *American Documentation,* 20(3), 1969, pp. 186-197.

Krech, David : Behavioural Science. *In :* Rosner, Stanley and Abt, Lawrence (Ed): The Creative Experience, New York, Grossman Publishers, 1970.

Krikelas, J.: Information-seeking Behaviour : Patterns and Concepts, *Drexel Library Quarterly,* 19(2), 1983, pp. 5-20.

Krummel, D.W. (Ed.): Introduction to Trends in The Scholarly Use of Library Resources, *Library Trends,* 25(4), 1977, pp. 725-732.

Kuhlthau, Carol C.: Inside the Search Process : Information Seeking from the User's Perspective, *Journal of the American Society for Information Science,* 42(5), 1991, pp. 361-371.

Kyvik, S.: Motherhood and Scientific Productivity, *Social Studies of Science,* 20, 1990, pp. 149-160.

Ladendorf, J.M.: Information Flow in Science, Technology and Commerce : A Review of the Concepts of the Sixties, *Special Libraries,* 61(5), 1970, pp. 215-222.

Lancaster, F.W.: Information Retrieval Systems : Characteristics, Testing and Evaluation, 2nd ed., New York, Wiley, 1979.

Laski, H.J.: The Danger of Obedience and Other Essays New York : Harper and Brothers, 1930.

Lehman, H.C.: Age and Achievement, Princeton, N.J.: Princeton University Press, 1953.

Lehrer, Stanley : Leaders, Teachers and Learners in Academy : Partners in Educational Process. New York : Appleton Century Crafts, 1970.

Leupolt, Martin : The Information Need, Its Nature and Its Implementation, *International Forum on Information and Documentation,* 8(3), 1983, pp. 3-7.

Levitan, Karen B.: Information Resources As "Goods" in the Life Cycle of Information Production, *Journal of American Society for Information Science,* January, 1982, pp. 44-54.

Libbey, M.A. and Zaltman, G.: The role and distribution of written informal communication in theoretical high energy physics, American Institute of Physics, Report AIP/SDD-I, rev., 1967.

Lin, N. and Garvey, W.D.: Information Needs and Uses, *Annual Review of Information Science and Technology,* 7, 1972, pp. 5-37.

Line, M.B.: The Information Uses and Needs of Social Scientists : An Overview of INFROSS. *Aslib proceedings,* 23, 1971, pp. 412-434.

Lipow, Anne Grodzins : Teaching the Faculty to Use the Library : A Successful Programme of Indepth Seminars for University of California, Berkeley, Faculty. *In* : Stuart, Robert D. and Johnson, Richard D. (Eds.): New Horizons for Academic Librarians, New York : K.G. Saur, 1979.

Livingstone, Hugh : The University : An Organizational Analysis, Glasgow : Blackie, 1974.

Loosejes, Th. P.: On Documentation of Scientific Literature, Translated by A.J. Dickson, London : Butterworths, 1967, pp. 67-82.

Lowenthal, D. and Wason, P.C.: Academics and Their Writings. *Times Literary Supplement,* 24th June 1977, p. 782.

Lufkin, J.M. and Miller, E.H.: The Reading Habits of Engineers — A Preliminary Survey, *IEEE Transactions on Education,* E-9, 4, 1966, pp. 179-182.

Maberly, Sir Walter : The Crisis in the University, London : SCM Press, 1949.

Machlup, F.: Knowledge : Its Creation, Distribution, and Economic Significance, Princeton, New Jersey : Princeton University Press, 1980.

Machlup, F.: The Production of Knowledge in the United States, Princeton : New Jersey : Princeton University Press, 1962.

Machlup, F. and Mansfield, U : Study of Information, Interdisciplinary Messages, New York : Wiley/Interscience, 1983.

Mackinnon D.W. : Identifying and Developing Creativity, *Journal of Secondary Education,* 38, 1963, pp. 166-174.

MacKinnon, D.W.: The Nature and Nature of Creative Talent, *American Psychologist,* 17, 1962, pp. 484-495.

MacKinnon, D.W. : 'Personality Correlates of Creativity', A Paper Presented at the Second Conference in Thinking, National Education Association, Washington, 2-4 May, 1963.

MacKinnon, D.W.: What Do We Mean by Talent and How Do We Test for It ? The Search for Talent. New York : College Entrance Board, 1960.

Mackay, D.M.: Information, Mechanism and Meaning, Cambridge : Mass, MIT Press, 1969.

Mansfield, R.S. and Bure, T.V.: The Psychology of Creativity and Discovery, Chicago : Nelson-Hall, 1981.

Martin, Miles W. and Ackoff, Russell L.: The Dissemination and Use of Recorded Scientific Information, *Management Science*, 9, 1963, pp. 322-336.

Martin, P.: The Innovative Process and the Online Information Channel, *In* : Stern, B.T. (Ed.): Information and Innovation, Amsterdam, North-Holland, 1982.

Martyn, J.: Information Needs And Uses, *Annual Review of Information Science and Technology*, 9, 1974, pp. 3-23.

Martyn, J.: Literature Searching Habits and Attitude of Research Scientists, London : British Library, 1987. (British Library Research Paper 14).

Marzocco, Frank N.: Human Dimensions of Information Need. *In* : Debons, Anthony and Cameron, Willam J. (eds.): Perspectives in Information Science. Leyden, Noordhoff International Publishing, 1975, pp. 75-92.

McCarthy, J.: Information, *In* : Information : A Scientific American Book. San Francisco : W.H. Freeman and Company, 1966.

Mc Donough, A.M.: Information Economics and Management Systems, New York : McGraw Hill, 1963.

Mc Elvia, J.L. et. al.,: Relationship Between Creativity and Teacher Variability, *Psychological Reports,* 13, 1963.

Meadows, A.J.: Communication in Science, London : Butterworths, 1974.

Mednick, S.A.: The Association Concept of The Creative Process, *Psychological Reviews,* 69, 1962, pp. 220-232.

Menzel, H.: Informal Needs and Uses in Science and Technology, *Annual Review of Information Science and Technology,* 1, 1966, pp. 41-69.

Menzel, H. et al.: Formal and Information Satisfaction of The Information Requirements of Chemists : Interim Report, Columbia University, Bureau of Applied Research, 1966.

Menzel, H. et al. : Review of Studies in the Flow of Information Among Scientists, Vol. 2, Columbia University, Bureau of Applied Social Research, 1960.

Merrill, M.: Regular and Irregular Library Use by Faculty Members at Three Universities. Ph.D. Thesis, University of Pittsburg, 1979.

Mikhailov, A.L. Chernyl, A.I. and Gilyarevskii : (Informatics—New Name for the Theory of Scientific Communication) Nanko-technicheskaya infomatisya, No. 12, 1966 (English translation in *FID News Bulletin,* 17, 1967, pp. 70-74).

Mohsin's Presidential Address - VIII All-India Guidance Conference, Allahabad, 1963.

Morgan, D.N.: Creativity Today, *Journal of Aesthetic Art and Criticism,* 12, 1953, p. 24.

Nanun, Burt : User Needs for Information in 2000. *In :* Boaz, Martha : Strategies for Meeting the Information Needs of Society in the Year 2000, Little Colorado : Libraries Unlimited Inc., 1981.

Nauta, D.: The Meaning of Information, The Hague : Mouton, 1972.

Newman, Geoffrey : A Institutional Perspective On Information, *International Social Science* is *Journal*, 28(3), 1976, pp. 466-492.

Newman, P.M.: The Value of Information. Paper presented to ISS Annual Conference, Longhorough 13th-15th April, 1978.

Oettinger, A.G.: Information Resources, *Science,* 209, 1980, pp. 191-198.

Olaisen, J.L.: Towards A Theory of Information Seeking Behaviour Among Scientists and Scholars, Ph.D. Thesis, University of California, Berkeley, 1984.

Oldman, Christine : The Value of Information, Bradford, Yorkshire : MCB (Library Research) Limited, 1976.

Otten, K. and Debons, A.: Towards A Meta-science of Information : Informatology, *Journal of American Society for Information Science,* 21(1), 1970, pp. 89-94.

Pachevsky, T.: Problems of Information Services with Respect to Integration of Sciences, *Journal of American Society for Information Science,* 33, 1982, pp. 115-123.

Paisley, W.J.: The Flow of (Behavioural) Science Information. A Review of the Research Literature. Institute for Communication Research, Stanford University, 1965.

Paisley, W.J.: Information Needs and Uses, *Annual Review of Information Science and Technology,* 3, 1968, pp. 1-30.

Palmer, Judith : Scientists and Information : I. Using Cluster Analysis to Identify Information Style, *Journal of Documentation,* 47(2), 1991, pp. 105-129.

Palmer, J.M.P.: Factors Affecting Information Behaviour of Agricultural Research Scientists, Ph.D. Thesis, University of Sheffield, 1991

Paramesh, C.R.: Value Orientations of Creative Persons. *Psychological Studies*, 15(2), 1970, pp. 108-112.

Parker, D.H.: Schooling for Individual Excellence, London : Nelson, 1963.

Parnes, S.J.: Creativity : Developing Human Potential, *Journal of Creative Behaviour*, 5(1), 1971, pp. 19-35.

Pelz, D.C. and Andrews, F.M.; Scientists in Organisations, New York : John Wiley, 1966.

Petrarca, A.E. et al., (Eds.) : Information Interaction. Proceedings., of the 45th ASIS Annual Meeting, White Plains, New York : Knowledge Industry Publication Inc., 1982.

Prasher, R.G.: Information and Its Communication, *ILA Bulletin*, 23(3), 1987, pp. 95-118.

Prodrick, Gerald : The Peculiar and Complex Economic Properties of Information, *Canadian Journal of Information Science*, 5, 1980, pp. 89-92.

Raina, M.K.: Verbal and Non-verbal Creative Thinking Ability : A Study in Sex Differences, *Journal of Education and Psychology*, 29(3), 1971, pp. 175-179.

Rajagopalan, T.S. and Rajan, T.N.: Conventional and Non-coventional Document Sources-Gutenberg 2, *Library Science with a Slant to Documentation*, 21(2), 1984, pp. 99-108

Rajyalakshmi, D.: Barriers Between the Library Users and the Library Staff, *International Library Movement*, 10(4), 1988, pp. 151-155.

Raganathan, S.R. : Colon Classification, 7th edition : A Preview. Sarada Ranganathan Endowment. Bangalore : DRTC, 1969.

Ranganathan, S.R. : Prolegomena to Library Classification, Asia Publishing House, 1967.

Ranaganthan, S.R.: University Library : Then and Now, *Library Herald*, 6, 1963, pp. 61-69.

Rathswohl, Eugene J.: Information Utilization and User Initiative. *In* : Debons, A. (Ed.): Information Science in Action : System Design, Vol.1, The Hague : Martinus Nijhoff, 1983, pp. 120-126.

Rathswohl, Eugene J.: Nature of Information. *In* : Debons, Anthony and Cameron, William J. (Eds.): Perspectives in Information Science, Leyden : Noordhoff International Publishing, 1975, pp. 21-30.

Ravichandra Rao, I.K.: Quantitative Methods for Library and Information Science. New Delhi : Wiley Eastern Ltd. (1983).

Rawlinson, J.G.: Creative Thinking and Brain Storming, London : Gower, 1981.

Redmond, D.A. et al.: University Libraries and University Research, *College and Research Libraries,* 33(6), 1972, pp. 447-453.

Reppo, Aatto, J.: The Dual Approach to the Value of Information : An Appraisal of Use and Exchange Value. *Information Processing and Management,* 22(5), 1986, pp. 373-383.

Revill, D.H.: 'Availability' As a Performance Measure for Academic Libraries, *Journal of Librarianship,* 19(1), 1987, pp. 14-30.

Rhodes, M.: An Analysis of Creativity, *Phi Delta Kappan,* 42, 1961, pp. 305-310.

Roe, Anne : A Psychological Study on Physical Scientists, *Psychological Monograph,* 43, 1951, pp. 121-239.

Rohde, N.F.: Information Needs. *In* Simonton, Wesley (Ed.): Advances in Librarianship, Vol. 14, Orlando : Academic Press, 1986, pp. 49-73.

Rosenberg, V.: Factors Affecting The Preferences of Industrial Personel for Information Gathering Methods. *Information Storage and Retrieval,* 3(3), 1967, pp. 119-127.

Rosner, Stanley and Abt, Lawrence (Ed.) : The Creative Experience. New York : Grossman Publishers, 1970.

Rossman, J.: A Study of the Childhood, Education, and Age of 710 Inventors, *Journal of Patent Office Society*, 17, 1935, pp. 411-421.

Rothwell, R. and Robertson, A.B.: The Role of Communication in Technological Innovation, *Research Policy*, 2, 1973, pp. 204-225.

Rowley, J.E. and Turner, C.M.D.: The Dissemination of Information, London : Andre Dentsch, 1978.

Rudolph, Frederick : The American College and University : A History, New York : Alfred A. Knopf, 1968.

Ruth, M. and Hartley, James; Teaching and Learning in Higher Education. London : Harper and Row, 1984.

Rzasa, P.V. and Baker, N.R.: Measures of Effectiveness for a University Library, *Journal of the American Society for Information Science*, 23(4), 1972, pp. 248-253.

Rzasa, Philip. V. and Moriarty, John H.: The Types and needs of Academic Library Users : A Case Study of 6,568 Responses. *College and Research Libraries*, Nov. 1970, pp. 403-409.

Saracevic, T. et al.: Causes and Dynamics of User frustration in Academic Library, *College and Research Libraries*, 38, January, 1977, pp. 7-18.

Schachtel, E.G.: Metamorphosis : On the Development of Affect, Perception, Attention and Memory, New York : Basic Books, 1959.

Searle, J.: The Campus War, Harmondsworth, Middx : Penguin 1972.

Sellen, M.K. and Jirouch, J.: Perceptions of Library Use by Faculty and Students : A Comparison, *College and Research Libraries*, 45, July, 1984, PP. 259-267.

Sharma, K.N.: Dynamics of Creativity, Agra : National Psychological Corporation, 1979.

Shah, A.B. (Ed.) : Higher Education in India, Bombay : Lalvani Publising House, 1967.

Shera, J.H. : The Foundations of Education for Librarianship. New York : Becker and Hayes, 1972.

Shera, J.H.: Sociological Foundations of Librarianship, New York : Asia Publishing House, 1970.

Shera, J.H.: and Cleveland, D.B.: History and Foundations of Information, *Annual Review of Information Science and Technology*, 12, 1977, pp. 249-275.

Shinebourne, I.: User Needs, The New Technology and Traditional Approaches to Library Services, *Journal of Information Science*, 2, 1980, pp. 135-140.

Shreider, I.U.A.: On the Semantic Characteristics Information, *Information Storage and Retrieval*, 2(3), 1965, pp. 221-233.

Siegel, Sidney and Castellar, N. John, Jr.: Non-Parametric Statistics for the Behavioural Sciences, New York; McGraw Hill, 1988.

Singh, Didar : Scientific Creativity and Personality, Agra : National Psychological Corporation, 1981.

Singh, Sewa : Information Services in University Libraries in India, *International Library Movement*, 12(1), 1990, pp. 1-11.

Slater, M. and Fisher, P.: Use Made of Technical Libraries, Aslib occasional publication No. 2, Aslib, 1969.

Smith, A.: Information and Creativity, ASIS Meeting, 1981.

Simth, C.J. and Kragh, Ulf : Creativity in Mature and Old age, *Psychological Research Bulletin*, 15(7), 1975, pp. 1-17.

Australia, 1984.

University Grants Committee : Report of the Committee on Libraries, London : HMSO, 1967.

Uytterschant, L.: Literature Searching Methods in Social Science Research : A Pilot Enquiry, *American Behavioural Scientist*, 9, 1966, pp. 23-26.

Smyth, D. Mc Cormack : Structure for University Government to the Begining of the 20th Century, *Cited in* Ross, Murray G.: The University. New York : McGraw-Hill, 1976.

Sontheimer, Kurt : Prediction as The Aim And Problem of Modern

S

S

S

S

St

St

St

Sto

Sto

Sto

Sto